THE WRITER'S GUIDE TO VIVID SETTINGS AND CHARACTERS

THE WRITER'S GUIDE TO VIVID SETTINGS AND CHARACTERS

AN AMAZING DESCRIPTIVE THESAURUS ON WRITING DESCRIPTION

S. A. SOULE

FWT

The Writer's Guide to Vivid Settings and Characters (Book 3)
ISBN: 978-1530807901
Updated and Expanded Edition April 2016

Cover art by SwoonWorthy Book Covers

Copyright © 2015 S. A. Soule

The moral right of the author has been asserted.

Published by FWT

FWT appreciates its readers, and every effort has been made to properly edit this guidebook. However, typos do get overlooked. If you find an error in the text, please send us an email so the issue can be corrected. Thank you!

Typesetting services by BOOKOW.COM

For fiction writers who yearn to take their writing skills to the next level!

Contents

INTRODUCTION

Dear Writer,

I've been writing most of my life, and even though I've studied the craft for years, I still love developing my skills as a writer, and I'm assuming since you purchased this book that you do, too.

First I thought I'd share a little about myself...I have over fifteen years of experience on all sides of the publishing business. I was a Creative Writing major in college, and I once owned an eBook publishing company where I edited over a hundred manuscripts. Then I worked as a developmental editor for another publisher, and in the last five years, I've even had the honor of editing books for a number of successful authors.

In the past, I've been traditionally published, and through a small indie publisher, and I've even self-published some of my work. Currently, I've written eleven fiction novels and eight nonfiction titles, but it wasn't until 2015 that I became a bestselling author, and the road to success has been a long journey. Many of my books have spent time on the 100 Kindle bestseller lists and some of my fiction has been chosen as top picks in the "Best Paranormal Romance" categories at several prominent review sites.

In this writing and editing guide, I share some of the wisdom that I've gleamed from various workshops and online courses, along with the savvy advice from bestselling novelists and professional editors with whom I've had the pleasure to work with in the publishing industry. And this manual provides step-by-step instructions on ways to create lifelike characters and vivid settings that writers can easily and quickly apply to their own writing. Plus, I've included a few inspiring quotes as additional encouragement.

This manual is not a "grammar do or don't" because mine is not the best, so please don't contact the literary police. Writers should use these tips as an arsenal of creative knowledge to include in their writer's toolbox. My goal is always for writers to come away with stronger writing and editing abilities that they can utilize in their own stories and give their audience a more personal reading experience.

There are a ton of great writing books and helpful blogs out there, so I hope my small contribution to the craft inspires you!

Happy writing and revising,

S. A. Soule

WRITING DESCRIPTION

Quote: "Try to cut down on your adjectives and adverbs. Modifiers don't specify words as much as you might think. More often than not, they actually abstract a thought, so sentences that rely on modifiers for descriptive strength are building on faulty foundations. You'll be more successful if you instead find the verb that perfectly portrays the image you're envisioning. When you edit your work, spend considerable time scrutinizing your sentences to make sure the action maximizes full descriptive potential." —*editor and writer, Jon Gingerich*

If you've finished writing a novel or short story, then congratulations! That is a huge accomplishment to be very proud of, but now comes the revision work that will *really* make your story shine…

This book should help writers create dramatic scenes and illustrate how to craft a distinct and realistic world filled with three-dimensional characters, vivid locations, and naturalistic weather. Throughout this guide, writers will learn how they can use the five senses to arouse the reader's own senses of sight, touch, hear, smell, taste, and even feel. I'll illustrate ways a writer of any genre can revise description info-dumps to establish a mood that harmonizes nicely with the novel's storyline, and even how to craft unique descriptions of characters, locations, and climate.

Each chapter provides specific, practical tools to help make writing descriptions and crafting three-dimensional characters simple and fun, with plenty of illustrations to highlight each point.

The most important writing tools that I provide in this book are:

* The importance of using sensory details

* To expertly master showing vs. telling

* The impact setting can have on a story

* To effectively describe vivid characters

* How adding color and weather will strengthen description

Any fiction writer who has taken a creative writing course, or received a professional edit on their manuscript, or worked with a critique partner has undoubtedly heard these three words: *show, don't tell.*

In my very humble opinion, I believe that fiction is mostly about establishing a visceral, emotional connection between the character(s) and the reader. Two ways to do this is to have a strong "suspension of disbelief" within the storyline by ensuring the plot is plausible, and even more importantly, by *showing* instead of *telling.*

One of the best ways to do this is to use a Deeper POV, which in most cases creates vibrant and dramatic images within the reader's mind that deeply immerses them in your fictional world.

Every writer has their strengths and weaknesses. Personally, I love writing descriptions of places, buildings, characters, and objects in great detail. I have fun finding new ways to add color and realism and the five senses to most of my scenes. But the majority of writers that I've worked with forget to include any details regarding the setting. While I'm reading and critiquing their work, I'm not connecting to the characters or the story, if I can't envision where a character is in a scene or their surroundings.

Description isn't optional in fiction. Every scene should include some details pertaining to the character's environment.

For instance, if a new scene starts with two characters talking, but there's no mention where the scene takes place or where the characters are, then it leaves me with a weak visual. Writers don't need to go into too much detail, but some is helpful in order to cement the scene and keep the characters from seeming as though they're just floating around in space instead of being firmly anchored to the fictional world where they exist.

I believe that if you make your settings original, they'll propel your story forward, infuse your fictional world with mood and atmosphere, and add the powerful flavor of emotion that agents/editors demand and readers enjoy.

In the early drafts of a manuscript, *telling* is expected. It is more important to get the story finished and the plot holes filled in, then to worry about if a writer is *showing* enough. It is during the revision stage of later drafts (more like draft five or six) when it's time to polish the settings and start checking for red flags of *telling* throughout the narrative.

Writers should want readers to experience the story through the senses of their characters. And by engaging the five senses, it helps readers connect more closely with the character's experience. Shallow sentences with filter words will have the opposite effect.

Please compare these descriptive examples...

SHALLOW: I <u>touched</u> the dress to <u>feel</u> the fabric.

SHOWING: My fingers caressed the silky fabric.

Notice the difference between the shallow description and the more vivid "showing" one?

If you're going to describe how something tastes, sounds and looks, then you can leave out how it feels and smells. You never want to assault your reader's senses, or they will skip ahead to get back to the action.

Please compare the next two examples...

SHALLOW:

When Scott <u>heard</u> the growling <u>sound</u>, he <u>looked</u> down and <u>saw</u> a large dog blocking the trail. He <u>knew</u> it would attack if he moved. Scott <u>felt</u> a sense of <u>terror</u> build in his heart.

SHOWING:

Scott halted at the warning growl. Standing in front of him was a large dog, flashing its teeth. He stifled the girlish shriek that leaked from his lips with one hand. His heart jackhammered in his chest as he took a stumbling step backward.

***

In the second example, you can imagine much more vividly the dog and Scott's emotional response. It is always better to attempt to make your scene unique by inserting some of the five senses into the narrative.

Throughout this guide I'll be discussing how writers can enhance elements of a story by incorporating a description of the locations, landscapes, and the characters in each scene. And I offer several simple techniques for creating sensory details to enhance the world-building.

*Note: Some topics mentioned in this book are also illustrated and discussed in my other guidebooks, *The Writer's Guide to Character Emotion* and *The Writer's Guide to Deep POV*.

DEEPER POV

No matter what genre you write, fiction writers should learn how to craft descriptions like a seasoned pro. World-building isn't easy, but creating original depictions of characters, locations, weather, and mood can greatly enhance anyone's writing.

Evocative settings are more effective and compelling when they're visible, auditory, olfactory, and tactile. And character descriptions are much more visual and lifelike when they have unique physical attributes.

That's why sensory details can enhance any setting through the descriptive use of smells, colors, textures, sounds, and the sense of touch/feel. A descriptive writer can trigger in the reader any of the five senses with evocative specifics.

The Deep POV method can be used in a lot of different ways besides the obvious ones, like *show emotions* or just *getting inside a character's head*. It can also aid in describing characters and crafting vivid settings through sensory details. Writers just need to understand *how* and *when* to apply it.

Showing merely means allowing the reader to deeply experience things for themselves, through the viewpoint and perception of a character. Deep POV is just describing everything that your character is feeling, observing, and identifying, along with whatever they're seeing, hearing, touching, and smelling, etc.

Creating vivid settings isn't easy. Most of my critique partners and the other writers with whom I work with tend to skip including any background scenery or description to their scenes. Or the descriptions are written too blandly and shallow. But characters need to be anchored to their settings and readers need visual images to envision the world in which you've created.

Often times, shallower writing (telling) occurs when a writer uses too many adverbs, other verbs, phrases, and adjectives to describe something, which could be considered "telling" the reader information about the characters or setting in a nondescript way. In fiction, verbs should carry the weight of the description, but using too many "ly" adverbs can deaden the writing.

If writers want to make a sentence have greater impact, then I suggest that they use a Thesaurus and search for the most dramatic, powerful verbs they can find.

Please compare these two sentences…

SHALLOW: Vaugh walked into the restaurant.

SHOWING: Vaughn sauntered into the restaurant.

Notice the difference between the shallow description and the more vivid "showing" one?

While the verb "walked" is okay to use in a sentence, it is rather flavorless. The second example *shows* the reader a much more vivid image of Vaughn entering the room.

I feel that the main reason writers are often cautioned against using adverbs is that many writers overuse them in descriptive sentences when a stronger verb would work better.

Descriptive details in a setting allows sensory recreations of experiences for our readers. In other words, description engages the senses and paints a more vivid image. Great description encourages readers to imagine a graphic setting or a sensory experience that allows the reader to transport themself into your fictional world. Writing that lacks description is in danger of being ambiguous or exceedingly generic.

To help me write tangible settings, I have created a folder (Description Docs) on my computer that is stuffed with files that I can reference with descriptive phrases, words, paragraphs, and scenes. Each file is simply labeled and easy to find. I have files categorized under: "Description – town or city" and "Description – fog – mist – dew" and "Description – bedroom" and so forth. They come in handy as I'm drafting a novel.

To encourage and help other fiction writers to craft stunning scenes and lush settings, I have included references from my own personal database of descriptions in this guidebook.

Why is setting and description so important?

The significance of adding description to your scenes means that you're using a Deeper POV and constructing dramatic, believable settings for your characters, *and* your readers.

For example, below is a short description of the heroine's bedroom in my novel, *Beautifully Broken* to give writers an idea on a short yet vivid description.

Please carefully examine this paragraph...

With the lights on, my gaze took in the cluttered space: the black-painted wall behind the bed covered with random poems, song lyrics, and cutouts from magazines. I yawned and plopped sideways on the iron-frame bed, rumpling the pink comforter that matched the curtains and fuzzy, circular rug under the desk. My swinging heel hit something solid. *The trunk.* I had forgotten...

That scene was vivid enough that it gives the reader a clear picture of the teen girl's bedroom in their mind.

When book reviewers use expressions like: "dramatic scenes," or "haunting imaginary," or "vivid prose" to describe the writing, what they're really stating is that the writer has succeeded at a Deeper POV, which we will go over in the next several chapters.

Throughout this guide, I have included examples to demonstrate how writers can avoid narrative distance in easy to grasp methods that can instantly improve anyone's writing.

*Please note that while all of the examples in my guidebooks have already been used (mostly in my own published novels and short stories), but you can turn almost any of these Deep POV examples into new, unique phrases that fit your own stories. The purpose of the examples that I provide are to get your own creativity flowing enough to come up with innovative ways to describe your characters and settings in your own distinctive style.

Now turn the page and get ready to be inspired!

SHOW DON'T TELL

Quote: "Description is often necessary to let your readers know where the characters are in the story. In TV and movies, a change of scene is often signaled by a brief shot of the place from the outside. Unless you are writing a graphic novel, you will need words to let your readers know where the characters are. Sometimes you can skip this by just having a phrase such as "3 p.m. Wednesday, OK Corral" at the top of a scene, but even then you may want to add words describing the dust, the tumbleweeds and the acrid smell of gun smoke." —*author, Victoria Grossack, Writing World*

It can often be a struggle for writers to figure out how much detail or description in a scene is too much or not enough.

The contrasts of showing vs. telling:

Telling is when a writer provides the reader with direct facts, or explains a situation, or offers important information in relation to the storyline in a straightforward manner. This approach is considered passive writing that summarizes events that aren't really significant to the plot, but they are necessary to fill in plot holes or get the info across quickly to keep the story moving forward.

The best reason to "tell" is simple conciseness.

For instance, if an event or object depicted is somewhat insignificant to the plot, a writer should only mention it in a short paragraph or sentence. (Or if it's really irrelevant, a writer should consider omitting it.)

Also, *telling* is an outdated way of storytelling with info-dumps that can bore the modern-day reader.

Showing is a way of dramatizing and *digging deeper* into a scene to make it come alive for the reader. It vividly conveys more of a visual for the reader through visceral, impactful, and evocative writing that allows them to effortlessly imagine the story-world, as well as the characters you've created. A Deeper POV is considered active writing, but it is typically more wordy and descriptive, but please do not let that hinder you from using it.

Also, *showing* can be conveyed through the author's use of language "voice," through the syntax and word choices. (I go into much more detail about character "voice" and a writer's narrative style in book two, *The Writer's Guide to Deep POV*, if you're interested.)

Effective descriptive writing includes many vivid sensory details that paint a picture and appeals to all of the reader's five senses when appropriate. Emotive descriptions often include figurative language such as intriguing similes and metaphors to help put a vivid image into the reader's mind. And descriptive scenes can also depict the feelings of the characters, and give a sense of *mood* to places or objects.

Please look at one example below (not terribly original)…

SHALLOW: The sun was setting and it was getting dark.

That sentence is a form of *telling*, and although the sentence states a fact, it gives a rather weak visual.

Here's the revised version that reveals (shows), instead of tells…

SHOWING: Long shadows yawned and stretched as the sun sunk below the horizon.

Now ask yourself: which description was more powerful and visual?

Now, I'm not suggesting that a writer show or describe *everything* in great detail because that would be overwriting and create pacing issues. The key is to understand the difference so writers can intelligently decide when to *show* and when to just *tell*. Finding a balance is necessary.

Detailed descriptions trigger a reader to feel, hear, taste, and even smell a scene, and become deeply connected with the images and experiences being recreated by the writer and described by the characters. There are many different ways that descriptive writing can be included in a story.

Here are a few easy to master tips on evocative writing to enhance your settings and character descriptions:

1) Writers should try to reduce as many filtering references as they can from their writing. Words such as *felt, saw, heard, smelled, tasted,* or *noticed,* etc. that tell the reader what the narrator felt or saw or heard instead of describing it with sensory details.

2) Be more specific when describing places, settings, people, clothing, objects, cars, etc. so you don't create a weak visual. By writing with precise and detailed words, and avoiding vagueness, writers will remove most of the "tells" from a story and breathe new life into any scene.

3) One way to rid your fiction of shallow writing is to use the "look through the camera lens" method, which is an excellent tool for helping writers begin to notice any *telling* within a manuscript.

Imagine this: the character is standing behind the camera, and everything in the scene is perceived through that POV character's eyes, and then reported to the reader through their perspective.

But the camera doesn't use all of the senses, like sounds, touch (the way something feels), smells, temperatures, or tastes. In addition, interior-dialogue—the character's internal thoughts and emotions—cannot be viewed by a camera, and so it is not (usually) considered telling.

There are times when *telling* is simply necessary, so it shouldn't be completely removed from your manuscript because that would be impossible and cause some of the prose to become particularly awkward. However, my advice is this: if you can rewrite the sentence and *show* instead, then do it. If some of the time you can't, then go ahead and leave the *telling* version in the scene.

In the next several chapters, I'll discuss how to describe your characters in vibrant details that will give your readers a clear image of the people populating your fictional world.

CHARACTER DESCRIPTION

Quote: "The description of a new character who has just entered your story having "big brown eyes and frizzy black hair" or "ginger hair that cascaded down her shoulders and eyes the color of jade." No matter how creative you get, describing a person according to his or her hair and eye color is A) Lazy B) Boring C) Ineffective D) Not memorable. *Really*—does telling you a woman has brown eyes and frizzy black hair give you ANY sense of what she looks like? Does it reveal anything unique about her that doesn't apply to 500,000 other people? Does it reveal anything about her character? Nay, nay and nay. And adding an age doesn't help much either." *—author, Megan Ward*

This chapter focuses on ways that writers can describe a character's physical appearance though a Deeper POV. While some writers might prefer to have minimal character descriptions, because they'd rather the reader imagine a characters' appearance in their own way, too little depictions can be confusing, too.

How you ever read a book and visualized the main character as a lanky, brown-haired nerd, only to discover fifty pages into the story that the character was a brawny, tan, blond guy?

Writers should describe the characters as early as possible in a manuscript, but avoid creating a boring list of attributes by using weaker descriptive words.

Description can be tough to write and so many writers neglect to add physical attributes to the narrative. Now, I know some of you will argue that other published writers do this, but I feel that *some* description of your characters is vital to a story.

Like so many writing techniques, it is always a good idea to have a balance of both *telling* and *showing* when describing a character's facial features. I recommend blending in movement, introspection, and an emotional reaction or impression whenever describing a character for the first time.

Please study this first example, where the sentence is *telling*...

SHALLOW:

Byron Evatt had ginger hair that looked greasy and he had a round face with brown eyes. He had a short body and wore old-fashioned clothing. He walked to the table on stunted legs.

Here is the revision, where same information is *shown*...

SHOWING:

Byron Evatt's greasy, ginger hair hung slack in his pudgy face. He brushed the strands out of his brown eyes, and took quick steps on stubby legs toward the table. His height and clothing resembled a dwarf from a child's fairy-tale.

Wasn't that second description much more visual?

Keeping the details very specific is one great way to improve character descriptions.

While a writer is describing their characters, only choose details that form the clearest, most informative impact. One or two relevant details such as, clothing, a distinct feature (like a mole or scar or broken nose), or a quirky characteristic can reveal more about the character effectively than a long, detailed summary.

Another way to vividly depict a character is to focus on distinctive characteristics that highlight their unique personality, such as biting their fingernails (although this is getting cliché), or a missing a limb from an accident, or a wandering eye, or a nervous twitch.

When I describe my own characters, I usually focus on one dominant feature or personality trait because it will give readers a more vivid image in their minds. For instance, when I write about the heroine of my paranormal romance series, Shiloh, I describe her scarred arm to give her an extra layer of realism, but it does play a huge part in her destiny and the ongoing storyline, so I do mention it more than once throughout the narrative.

However, writers should try not to do an info-dump of character description that slows the pace. Because there's no need to overload the scene with too many physical descriptions or disclose all the personality traits or details in the same scene.

Also, be careful of mentioning an object or physical trait more than three times in a story because then the reader will think it has some importance to the plot, and it if it doesn't, then there is no need to mention it multiple times. For instance, in an early draft of one of my novels, I mentioned that the heroine had a belly-ring at least four or five times whenever I was describing her clothing. Then a reviewer made a nasty comment about it being overkill…and, well, it was. So I removed almost every mention of it and focused more on her ugly scar, which did have a significant connection to the plot.

The same goes for details of physical description. If a writer describes a character's freckled skin, only do it once or twice at most.

PHYSICAL ATTRIBUTES

Creative storytelling that effectively uses evocative writing and sensory details allows a reader to do more than merely read the words on a page. While there are many different uses of description, most readers need vibrant images and physical details to envision fictional characters.

So I suggest that writers allow their descriptions to multitask by also revealing (*show* rather than *tell*) more about a character's personality and background. But if writers use clichéd, colorless descriptions, it can be too generic and the depictions don't really help the reader get a clear image of the characters. So try to avoid using descriptors that simply label a character, *short, fat, young, old,* or *ordinary,* which do not create a vivid picture in the reader's mind.

I have included some more examples below to show writers what I mean.

Here's an excerpt from *A Drink Before the War* by Dennis Lehane that combines a character's description with a glimpse of their personality.

Sterling Mulkern was a florid, beefy man, the kind who carried weight like a weapon, not a liability. He had a shock of stiff white hair you could land a DC-10 on and a handshake that stopped just short of inducing paralysis.

***

Here's an excerpt taken from *Fifty Shades of Grey* by E. L. James that combines a character's description with dialogue and introspection. Please examine this example…

He extends a long-fingered hand to me once I'm upright. "I'm Christian Grey. Are you all right? Would you like to sit?"

So young—and attractive, *very* attractive. He's tall, dressed in a fine gray suit, white shirt, and black tie with unruly dark copper colored hair and intense, bright gray eyes that regard me shrewdly.

***

Here's an excerpt taken from my novella, *Pride, Prejudice, and Vampires* that merges a character's description with an emotional reaction and introspection…

Within the high-ceiling room stood a man with wavy dark hair that inexplicably made Elizabeth Bennet's heart slam against her ribcage. He wore a perfectly fitted, inky black tailcoat, which covered a blood-red brocade waistcoat, cream-colored shirt, and silken black cravat around his neck. His posture was ramrod straight and his chin slightly lifted as if he was looking down his nose at the other guests. Elizabeth studied his profile. Although he seemed familiar, she couldn't place him, certainly not from this angle.

***

Here's an excerpt taken from *Flawless* by Lara Chapman that merges setting description, along with character description. Please examine this example...

The once-buzzing classroom freezes. Standing in the doorway is the hottest guy I've ever laid eyes on. Golden brown hair cut just short enough to be stylish and a body I've only seen on television. Honest to God, the room has fallen dead silent while he looks at his schedule and compares it to the number on the door....

When he looks up and finds everyone staring, he glances behind himself to see what they're looking at. Realizing he's the center of attention, he smiles, upping the charm of his rugged good looks when his slightly imperfect teeth are revealed.

***

Here's an excerpt taken from *Third Grave Dead Ahead* by Darynda Jones that describes a character's description, along with their state of mind. Please examine this example...

His tall, thin frame seemed to sag just a bit. His blond hair looked barely combed, and his bloodshot eyes were lined with a purplish hue. And not a pretty purple either. It was that dark grayish purple that depressed people wear.

***

Here's an excerpt taken from *The Likeness* by Tana French that mixes a character's description with an emotional reaction. Please examine this example...

I'd been expecting someone so nondescript he was practically invisible, maybe the Cancer Man from *The X Files*, but this guy had rough, blunt features and wide blue eyes, and the kind of presence that leaves heat streaks on the air where he's been.

***

By trying to create meaningful, descriptive prose, it will naturally move the story forward and convey a richer experience for your reader.

DESCRIPTIVE POV

Quote: "Thin description leaves the reader feeling bewildered and nearsighted. Over description buries him or her in details and images. The trick is to find a happy medium. It's also important to know what to describe and what can be left alone while you get on with your main job, which is telling a story."
—bestselling author, Stephen King

The best technique to describing characters is to present just enough relevant details to help your reader instantly "see" the character in their mind without doing an info-dump, because the right blend of description and introspection, along with engaging all the senses through a Deeper POV, can create a stronger image for the reader.

Telling descriptions create weak illustrations that can leave the reader grappling for a visual and feeling disconnected from the characters and the scene.

One way to describe a character is start with the head-to-toe method. Start off by describing the upper part of the body, like the face and head, and then continue downward until you get to the legs or feet. Try to weave into the depiction any features that will give the reader the most effective visual, such as mentioning the hairstyle and color, then the eye shape and color, followed by any distinguishing facial features.

When describing a character, ask yourself: What sets this character apart from others in my narrative?

For instance, *does the character have freckles? A dimpled chin? Moles? A missing an eye? Scars? Birthmarks? Crooked teeth? A strong schnoz? Round, flush cheeks? Cute dimples? A wide Joker-smile? Big forehead? High-cheekbones? Thin lips?*

Next, move onto the chest and arms, and then you can even add in the height and weight.

The description doesn't need to be too long or too detailed. A vivid visual description is clear, illuminating, and creative. Having more than a page of complex exhaustive descriptions of characters is unnecessary, and might bore the reader. Also, avoid using any scientific verbiage in your descriptions. If you want your character description to be effective and memorable, it is a good idea to strive to make it as unique as possible.

I have included two illustrations below. The first example is considered shallower writing, and the revised version is *showing* the reader with sensory details and a closer POV.

Here are two examples I crafted to clarify how to describe a fictional character...

SHALLOW:

She noticed that Brock Massey had long black hair and thin features and blue eyes. Brock also had tan skin with a large nose and a sturdy-looking frame.

SHOWING:

Brock Massey's long black hair hung loose around his bony face. His clear blue eyes stood out in contrast to his tan skin, which had the look of a man who spent a lot of time outdoors. Brock rubbed his bold nose that dominated his meaty features, then sneezed. When he ducked under the doorway to enter the room and grab a tissue, his robust body lumbered forward like a gentle giant.

Notice the differences between the shallow description and the more vivid "showing" one?

I have included some more examples on describing physical characteristics from other authors. Here's an excerpt taken from *Harry Potter and the Sorcerer's Stone* by J. K. Rowling. Please examine this example...

He was a big, beefy man with hardly any neck, although he did have a very large mustache. Mrs. Dursley was thin and blonde and had nearly twice the usual amount of neck, which came in very useful as she spent so much of her time craning over garden fences, spying on the neighbors.

Another example from author J. K. Rowling ...

A giant of a man was standing in the doorway. His face was almost completely hidden by a long, shaggy mane of hair and a wild, tangled beard, but you could make out his eyes, glinting like black beetles under all the hair.

Here is another example on ways to describe a character. This excerpt is from *Deadly Cool* by Gemma Halliday that illustrates a character's description. (*I love this visual!*)

Please examine this example…

I thought I vaguely recognized him from school, though he wasn't in any of my classes. His hair was dark, cropped close and a little spiky on top. He wore unrelieved black from head to toe—black pants, black T-shirt, jet-black hair—and I wasn't sure, but it looked like he was even wearing black eyeliner. The whole effect gave him a dark, dangerous vibe, intensified by the way he was towering over us.

***

If a writer sprinkles the physical characteristics of a character, such as descriptions of their clothing, age, hair and eye color, height, weight, visible scars, or nationality into a scene, it will avoid becoming an info-dump.

And I strongly suggest that each time a new character is introduced to the storyline, that the writer provides the reader with a visual illustration. Now, it doesn't have to be a lengthy description of the character, a few well-placed descriptive details should be enough.

This next excerpt is from *Body Language* by Suzanne Brockman that illustrates a character's description. (A great author to read if you'd like to study how to write in Deep POV.)

Please examine this description…

She stared at him, trapped by the smoky vehemence in his eyes. He was still mere inches away from her, and she could see tiny flecks of brown and green mixed in with the almost aquamarine blue. His pupils were surrounded by a tiny ring of gold. "You have beautiful eyes, McCade," she breathed, and as she watched, his pupils dilated.

***

I have included an excerpt from my novel, *Lost in Starlight*, to show writers the difference between "voice" and bland narration. The first one is an early draft that has shallow writing with lots of *telling* and hardly any Deep POV or sensory details. (The words considered filtering references are underlined.)

Please compare these examples…

SHALLOW:

I open my locker and looked at him. Hayden was a tall guy and he looked more like a man. His features looked different, though—because he had a nice body. I notice that he has a bag, and I see drumsticks inside his pocket. I lift my hand to wave at him hesitantly because I feel unsure. I notice that he does not wave back. I see him looking at me with his different looking eyes.

Now, this second scene has been rewritten to clearly reveal "voice" in the speech, internal-thoughts, and the narrative, and it even shows a Deeper POV.

Please compare this revised example…

SHOWING:

While opening my locker, I'm suddenly aware that Hayden's blatantly staring at me. Hard to miss. He's like a man among boys, at least in his flawless physique. His messenger bag is in one hand, and drumsticks stick out of his back pocket. I lift my hand in a hesitant little wave. He doesn't return my gesture. Hayden just continues gazing at me through those thick lashes that frame his unique eyes.

* * *

Could you notice the difference?

Each scene presents the same scenario, but how the character relates the description to the reader is *shown* through the words used to convey the character's "voice." I encourage writers to revise any character descriptions with their own stories through "voice" and a Deeper POV.

SHALLOWER WRITING

When a writer describes a character's physical appearance, sometimes detailed facts about their features, such as height and weight, are not quite visual enough.

Writers need to make all characters as three-dimensional as possible, so that the reader sees them as real people. One way to do that is apply the Deep POV method, which will effectively give each of your characters a distinctive "voice" that comes across in your narrative. Choose your words carefully, because they will reveal a lot about your character and vividly *show* their unique voice.

Here are two examples I crafted to clarify how to describe a character...

SHALLOW (*and too much passive writing*):

Cyrus was standing on the other side of the dining room, and Brenda was watching him while he was greeting the dinner guests. He looked unremarkable. He was bald, except for a thick mustache. He was fat and wore a blue suit. When Brenda saw him remove his jacket, she saw sweat marks on the underarms of his shirt that she thought looked gross.

Here is the revision, where same information is *shown* with "voice"...

SHOWING:

Cyrus stood on the other side of the dining room, greeting the dinner guests. He reminded Brenda of a used car salesmen, someone kind of shady with beady eyes. His baldhead shone under the glow of the chandelier, and a piece of brie was wedged in his bushy mustache. When he waddled around the oak table, his fat stomach jiggled like a jolly Santa, barely hidden behind a blue double-breasted suit. When he shrugged off his jacket, big, nasty sweat marks had stained his underarms.

Notice the differences between the shallow description and the "showing" one?

These next three excerpts were all from my young adult novel, *Destiny Disrupted.* Each one illustrates how writers can describe a character through Deeper POV and "voice" and emotional reactions. This first scene is where the main character is attacked by some visiting demons.

Please closely examine this first example...

In those terrible, heart-pounding seconds, we just stared at each other. *Esael?* My stomach lurched. No way. It couldn't be. This guy must be a distant cousin who'd come to exact vengeance.

Two shorter demons appeared, separating from the shadows and marching toward us. They were all the same type, with scaly reptilian skin, powerful builds, and long arms ending in claw-like hands. Their black hooded robes dragged on the ground.

***

This second scene is where the main character is helped by a fallen angel. Please closely examine this next example…

Raze—the newest and youngest leader of the *Forsaken*—crossed his arms over his chest. He stood over six-feet tall and resembled one of the Norse gods, but definitely more Loki than Thor. Even his outfit screamed dark and mysterious: ragged jeans, black T-shirt, and scuffed tactical boots. Hair the shade of polished coal rested on slim shoulders. Moonlight caught a glint of the iridescent wings fluttering behind him, feathers that appeared to be molded from fragments of night sky.

Totally crush-worthy, if you liked nearly perfect guys without many flaws. And the wings were a bonus if you didn't like flying coach.

Not that I was drooling over him or anything. Not when I had a smoking hot boyfriend that I was totally into. Honest.

***

This last scene weaves the physical attributes throughout the dialogue to avoid an info-dump.

Please closely examine this third example…

I walked across Redwood High's campus toward the cafeteria with my best friend Ariana Parsons and my former frenemy

Brittany Lau-Witheridge, our feet crunching over the leaf-strewn walkway.

Brittany lifted her fur-lined hood over her head. "So are all the wolfy-football-jerks going to behave now?"

"As long as the boys keep guzzling the nonviolence potion Shiloh's mom makes them drink," Ariana replied. "Which should help them stay out of trouble."

"One can only hope." Brittany untangled strands of black hair caught in one of her silver necklaces. She had distinct Asian features and her slim figure was clad in a ruffled blouse, tight designer jeans, and kitten heels, all of which screamed *money*. If she sold that outfit, she could probably buy my house with the proceeds.

Beside Brittany's slender frame, Ariana's body seemed extra voluptuous, and a light breeze lifted her curly blond hair from her shoulders.

***

Here is an excerpt taken from *Opposing Sides* by author CM Doporto. Please examine this example…

I stepped out of the elevator and immediately caught a glimpse of my drop-dead gorgeous fiancé. He sported a pair of jeans and a blue and white striped sweater. My eyes traveled over his body. I couldn't wait to touch the muscles hiding underneath his layers of clothes.

***

A clever writer applying the Deep POV method can learn to skillfully tuck the physical characteristics into the narrative by lacing it through action and dialogue. Just remember that writers should always strive to *show* instead of *tell*.

FACIAL FEATURES

Quote: "Deep POV, with all its jam-packed emotion, grabs you with a hard-hitting emotional punch! In this way, our writing is never tame. It has the fire and guts and spirit—the life all its own—to succeed in this crazy industry we're working in. So what we need to do is live the story so deeply that emotion will flow." —*author, Melissa James, WOW! Women on Writing*

When writers describe a character, it is important to be as descriptive as possible without making it read like an inventory of attributes. Don't just tell the reader that John was handsome or Jane was ugly, but try to *show* it through a Deeper POV.

Let's start with a few features that writers could use to describe a character that might be considered less than attractive.

List of unattractive character features might be:

Clothes: baggy, cheap, mismatched colors, socks with sandals, ratty, stained, etc.

Face: bleached, bleak, bony, emaciated, chubby, round, rough, etc.

Nose: long, big nostrils, crooked, hook, bulbous, bulbous, pointy, etc.

Lips: thin, colorless, uneven, cracked, dry, flat, etc.

Eyes: beady, squinty, bloodshot, dull, hooded, rheumy, sunken, etc.

Hair: tangled, unwashed, unevenly cut, frizzy, etc.

Body: overweight, flabby, puny, weak, boney, meaty, etc.

Ears: pointy, small, large, droopy, floppy, stick-out, etc.

Chin: protruding, pointy, double-chin, etc.

Complexion: wrinkly, acne, stretch marks, scars, warts, rough, veiny, etc.

Teeth: crooked, missing teeth, pointy, large, chipped, over-bite, yellow, etc.

Eyebrows: bushy, heavy, thick, shaggy, thin, etc.

That short list should give writers some clever ideas on how to describe an unattractive character in their fictional story. However, writers should try not *tell* the reader what a character looks like in a generic, nonspecific way.

Here are two examples I crafted to show how to vividly describe a character...

SHALLOW:

She was ugly. Her hair was twisted into coils that fit around her lengthy face. She had green eyes that were too close together, and her nose was hooked. She smiled and I saw yellow stains on her teeth. Her round, short body was covered in black, plain clothing.

That shallow description is too generic, and it doesn't help the reader to clearly envision the character.

SHOWING:

Her dreadlocks outlined her long face like Medusa's head of snakes. Her moody emerald eyes were set too close together, and her nose hooked downward. When she smiled, it revealed yellowish stains on her crooked teeth. Her drab, dark clothing hung off her stout frame like ill-fitting curtains.

Notice the differences between the shallow description and the more vivid "showing" one?

Now here's some more inspiration for describing the characters in your fictional world. I put together a few key features that writers could use to describe a character that might be considered attractive.

List of an attractive character's features might be:

Clothes: tailored, expensive, trendy, sporty, flashy, chic, etc.

Face: chiseled, angular, delicate, oval, feminine, arresting, masculine, etc.

Nose: upturned, aquiline, refined, aristocratic, defined, Romanesque, etc.

Lips: plump, sensual, firm, full, glossy, beautiful, etc.

Eyes: oval-shaped, exotic, dreamy, expressive, doe-eyed, brilliant, etc.

Hair: bouncy, shiny, silky, flowing, thick, velvety, soft, etc.

Body: slender, athletic, muscular, lithe, etc.

Ears: small, flat, cute, curving, etc.

Chin: angular, chiseled, square, cleft, etc.

Complexion: porcelain, bronzed, flawless, smooth, supple, etc.

Teeth: white, straight, pearly, toothy, perfect, etc.

Eyebrows: amber, arched, lifted, raised, waxed, plucked, shaped, etc.

***

That short list should give writers some clever ideas on how to describe a good-looking character.

Here are two examples I wrote to illustrate how to describe an attractive character...

SHALLOW:

She was beautiful. She had a shapely figure and her waist was tapered. She had a burnished complexion and arched eyebrows above big brown eyes. Her delicate ears peeked out from beneath black hair. She laughed and I noticed she had a cute button nose. A set of dazzling, white teeth (cliché) gleamed when she smiled with her plump lips.

SHOWING:

Her shapely figure was draped in a clingy red dress that accented her tiny waist. The sunlight struck her burnished skin giving it a warm glow, and her arched eyebrows framed a doe-eyed brown stare.

With graceful movements, she pushed loose strands of glossy, night-black hair behind her delicate ears. She smiled when she saw me, her heart-shaped lips lifting at the corners and revealing straight, white teeth. When she laughed, her cute button nose scrunched.

***

Rather than giving readers a long, meticulous description of a character's height, weight, facial features, and clothing, it's best to just show the "personality" of the character through a Deeper POV and lacing in some action and introspection.

A few well-chosen details will give the reader a clear visualize of your character. Then you can just let the readers imagine the rest themselves.

OVERWORKED CLICHÉS

Quote: "In an effort to dodge the "show, don't tell" bullet, a lot of writers have taken the external route in conveying the emotions of their character. As I've said before, there's Bad Telling, and there's Good Telling. Bad telling deals with you just stating a fact about your character and then taking all the fun out of reading for your audience. Good telling involves using story context and, more importantly, interiority, to paint a three-dimensional picture where you make your reader feel the story experience, but you don't exclude them from participating, either." —*Mary Kole, literary agent and blogger at kidlit.com*

One of the biggest challenges a lot of writers struggle with is describing something as *beautiful*—a sunrise, a flower, a landscape—without applying an overused cliché. Although writers want to craft vivid descriptions that are evocative and significant, they often wind up describing nouns, such as places, people, and things with phrases like "velvety soft" or "hauntingly beautifull." Sometimes writers don't even realize when they're using a cliché.

Writers can use adjectives to depict something, but descriptive adjectives that describe a noun or pronoun can become cliché as well. Most adjective phrases have been overused in fiction, such as *skin as white as snow*, or *twinkle in her/his eye*, or *tall, dark, and handsome*, or a *gleaming white smile*.

If writers use an adjective to describe a physical feature, they should make sure that the phrase is unique and creative. Because using an overworked cliché to describe a place, person (character), or item, a writer is actually conveying to the reader that they lack originality.

Clichés are vague, and these trite phrases can make a story seem boring.

Clichés make a writer appear lazy.

Clichés are a poor alternative for descriptive writing.

Too many overworked clichés can cause author intrusion and jolt the reader from the narrative.

Here are two longer examples that I wrote to show writers how to depict a character...

SHALLOW (overly descriptive and wordy):

Her very tall height towered over the other men. I thought she was a very big person because she had these wide birthing hips (cliché). Next, I noticed her dark complexion, very small ears, and little nose.

I watched her pause near a table. Her thin eyebrows frowned over her green eyes. When she saw her husband, the lady grinned, her pearl-white teeth (cliché) lit up her long face, in a megawatt smile (cliché). The woman had perfect red finger-nails that moved through her long brown hair. She had an attractive face and a graceful swan-like neck (cliché). Her pastel-pink lips looked soft as rose petals (cliché). I thought her stylish garments fit her giant frame like a glove (cliché), and I smelled an orange scent that came from her body.

Bland and boring, right? Showing is mainly in reference to replacing ambiguity. The first scene is vague and wordy, and not at all evocative or visually pleasing.

SHOWING:

Her Amazonian stature towered over the other men as she entered the room. Her wide hips swung with each step and her stylish dress hugged her incredible frame. Suddenly, I felt short and un-masculine in this woman's domineering presence. I couldn't help staring at her, and the way the soft candlelit glow gave her complexion a flawless, tannish hue.

She stopped near a table, and her forest-green stare swept the space, then both thinly plucked eyebrows slanted downward. Everything about her seemed exaggerated except her cherub ears and diminutive nose.

When she caught sight of her husband, she widely smiled with pink lips, displaying straight teeth. For a moment, she looked pretty and almost feminine. She raked red fingernails through her long, chestnut brown mane, the stands outlining her arresting face and revealing an elegant neck. As she moved past me, I inhaled a citrusy fragrance wafting from her skin.

Notice the differences between the shallow description and the more vivid "showing" one?

My advice is to substitute any stale phrases with something more original and imaginative.

If a number of clichéd writing gets overlooked by you and your editor, don't stress over it. No one can catch them all, but using a software program like "Editor" from Serenity-Software, or any online cliché finder to eliminate them might help.

If you find more than five clichés in your current manuscript, then I would revise them. Some are okay, but too many will create a red flag to book reviewers and readers that the work hasn't been fully polished enough.

FILTER WORDS

Quote: "Filtering words are generally words that you add to a sentence when you are trying to describe something that your character is experiencing or thinking. These can be sense words like *feel, taste, see, hear,* and *smell,* or variations thereof. Writers don't necessarily have to avoid these words, but they should be aware of the effect that they have on your prose. Rather than describing a sensation outright, you are distancing your reader from the sense that you are describing." —*young adult author, Corrine Jackson*

If a writer overuses filter words (shallow writing) it can remove the reader from the experience the character is describing and creates narrative distance. Anything that states the narrator's thought or mode of perception is considered "telling" the reader. If you can revise those sentences as much as possible, the POV will feel deeper and your descriptions and settings will be greatly enhanced.

In almost every scene, I think it's important to stay in Deep POV. One way is to try to reduce the number of filtering references. So rather than: "he/she felt," or "he/she see or saw," or "he/she hear or heard," or "he/she noticed," simply describe the emotion or thought or feeling through Deep POV.

I realize that writers cannot remove every occurrence of filtering, but they can revise those shallower words whenever possible. Just remember that Deep POV respects the reader's intelligence. Because writers that have a dull, unemotional narrative can often leave a reader feeling distanced and disconnected from the characters and not caring what happens to them.

To avoid filter words, a useful tool to help search out and eliminate repetitive or unproductive words is the FIND and RE-PLACE function in Microsoft Word. Either delete the weak word entirely or revise the sentence into actively showing. Alternatively, print the page and use a colored highlighter to single out needless words, and then re-edit the scene.

The problem is when writers consciously or unconsciously insert filter words into the narrative, it creates narrative distance. This issue is also known as author intrusion.

In my early drafts, I use a lot of filter words too, but I try to weed them out completely before my final draft. Once you start noticing them, they are simple to spot, and it becomes easier to stay in Deep POV by revising your narrative.

Let's review another example on how to create a vivid fictional character...

SHALLOW:

Camryn Chilton had shaggy brown hair and a thin, cheerful face. She had gray eyes and a birthmark under the right eye. For a woman, I thought she had a brawny frame.

SHOWING:

Camryn Chilton's generous mouth lifted into a friendly smile, making her gray eyes crinkle at the corners. Her shaggy brown hair framed a thin, pale face, and a slight birthmark under her right eye stained her cheekbone. She stepped forward, but her brawny frame barely fit through the front door.

Notice the differences between the shallow description and the more vivid "showing" one?

The shallower description is too generic, and it doesn't help the reader to clearly envision the character.

There are many, many different ways to write in a Deeper POV, and this guide is not meant as a strict rule. Remember, with any guides or advice on fiction writing, trust your own instincts. As you start to revise your own work, remember that it is easy to unintentionally violate the *show, don't tell* principle when you're writing an early draft.

SPECIFIC DETAILS

When you're writing descriptions strive to follow this advice...

Attempt to replace any vague details with a brand, or use a more specific word or verb whenever describing objects, clothes, people, buildings, cars, etc. It will keep writers in a Deeper POV and connect more with readers.

I recently went through one of my YA novels after I read this advice and it made such a difference in the heroine's "voice" and the story. I named all the streets, used more creative words to describe colors, laced in some brand names and fabrics to my clothing, and added model types to all my vehicles.

I included a few examples below to illustrate my point. Please analyze these two different sentences...

SHALLOW: I got into my car.

SHOWING: I hoped into my convertible BMW. (Replace all of the "car" words with the specific make or model)

Please review these two different examples...

SHALLOW: She slipped on a blouse.

SHOWING: She slipped on a white, ribbed tank, and over that she yanked on a red Abercrombie sweater. (Replace all of the "shirt" or "jeans" words with the specific brand or fabric)

Please study these two differing examples…

SHALLOW: The old house looked fancy and it had a few windows.

SHOWING: The lemon painted Georgian-style home had four rectangles of glass placed on the front side. The second-floor was decorated with cupolas and balconies, giving the exterior an elegant façade.

Please study these two different examples…

SHALLOW: I drove down the street and turned left at the light.

SHOWING: I shifted the Camry into drive and sped down Main Street, at the intersection I turned left onto Maple Drive before parking in the empty lot across from Starbucks.

After reading the "showing" examples, which ones do you think painted a more vivid picture for the reader? Getting some clear ideas for your own work yet?

Now describing a first-person narrator is a bit trickier, but not impossible if you have the tools.

This next excerpt is from my novel, *Lost in Starlight* and the scene illustrates how to lace "voice" with action and humor through the POV of a first-person narrator. Please examine this example…

Saturday night arrives, which means it's the evening of the big party. This also means I will soon be hanging with Hayden. Alone. Sort of.

I'm staring at my reflection in the mirror and trying to decide if I need to add a choker to my outfit. I'm wearing a red bowling shirt with black piping, with onyx shorts and suspenders, over black-and-white ripped stockings that rise above my knees. I slip on a pair of platform Mary Janes. My hair flows loose down my back, the purple highlights glossy under the lamplight.

"I look pretty good," I mutter, and glance at the heap of clothes on the bed.

Jinx peeks out from under a purple corset. No way am I going to change again. I've spent all evening rummaging through my closet, mostly driving myself crazy. Picking this outfit was hell, and I'm not going to search for something different.

The doorbell chimes. My date is here.

My palms start to sweat and my heart kicks into overdrive. I should've told him that I'd meet him there. Already I want to blow chunks and I haven't even seen Alien Boy yet.

My gaze roams over my reflection one last time. This is my last chance to add a necklace or touchup my makeup. Maybe I should wear boots instead of heels…

The doorbell rings again.

I had better get my butt moving before my brother answers the door and embarrasses the crap out of me. I grab my velvet handbag and dash downstairs.

***

Here is an excerpt taken from *Strange Angels* by Lilith Saintcrow. Please examine this example...

By the time I stamped down the stairs, I was already pissed off and getting worse. My favorite jeans weren't clean and I had a zit the size of Mount Pinatubo on my temple under a hank of dishwater brown hair. I opted for a gray T-shirt and a red hoodie, a pair of combat boots and no makeup.

***

Here is an excerpt taken from my book, *Beautifully Broken* (free to download from all major online book retailers for a limited time, if you'd like to support me reading a copy) that shows how to cleverly describe a first-person narrator...

I nodded and Ariana hugged me tightly, the sleeves of her ivory babydoll pullover wrapped around my body. Her hair smelled like honeysuckle, and the familiar scent made me feel instantly better, less jittery.

Looking at my best friend, I noted that we were total opposites. Not that I was shy, but I was thin compared to her, and my slight 5'6" frame made her voluptuous 5'2" figure seem excessive. Her delicate features, eyes as blue as the sky, curvaceous figure, and pale complexion—direct sunlight sometimes gave it this sparkly glow—were in complete contrast to someone like me who was composed of differing shades of brown. With my mix of Sioux and French heritage, I'd inherited high cheekbones, smooth olive skin, bronze eyes that dominated my face, and a flood of hair the shade of midnight.

Did I mention I was jealous of Ariana's porcelain skin and bigger boobs? *Ah, well, I still love her.*

***

This next passage was taken from my new adult novel, *Smash Into You*, and it should give you a pretty good idea on how to describe a first-person narrator...

Laughter seeped through the closed window and I stood, catching sight of my reflection in the glass, symmetrical features—plump lips, high cheekbones, tiny nose, cerulean eyes—and a head of long blonde hair. The window overlooked the courtyard and I sat on the sill, staring at the dark sky, while my breath fogged the glass. Girlish laughter rang out from the darkness below again and my heart squeezed painfully.

***

A word of warning...

Even though brand names can be useful in description, if they are overused, then they will distract the reader and might even annoy them. So don't go overboard using brand names to label every piece of clothing or product. The occasional use is fine, but most readers don't really care if a character wears Chucks while drinking a Coke and watching Netflix on his Kindle Fire.

Now I challenge you to rewrite a scene in your own novel or story and use clever ways to describe your amazing characters.

HAIR DESCRIPTION

This chapter is for hair description. Don't groan. Now, unless your characters are all bald, this list may come in handy.

Adding descriptions of hair may seem silly to some of you, but if you write young adult or new adult novels, it will add an extra layer of depth to your storyline. Teens often express themselves through fashion and hairstyles, so reference this chapter whenever you're stuck on physical attributes, like describing a character's hair.

And I think writers should at least give their readers a quick reference to each character's hair, either with color, length, style, or texture.

Also, strive to be specific. Don't just state that he/she has "blond hair" because it doesn't generate a clear image for the reader as much as stating the character had "long golden tresses." Powerful character descriptions can add flair to your descriptions, and create a sense of intimacy between your characters and readers.

Based on research done on facial features derived from Chinese medicine, a person's hair type can say a lot about their personality.

In Chinese medicine, all structures strive for balance, so if a character with wavy or curly hair likes to flat-iron their luscious strands to make them straight, it might be giving a character a sense of calmness.

Or if the character has red locks (even if the character colors their hair red), it could mean that they're a fun person, who is high-spirited, has a great sense of humor, and likes to keep things simple in his/her relationships.

Or a character with curly tresses would have a compassionate nature and a cheerful disposition. Research indicates that people with curls are very generous, but also have a fiery temperament. So there's also the likelihood that these characters can be quite the drama queens.

Or a character with thick, lustrous waves would be considered inventive and artistic. These characters could be deeply emotional, have high-energy, and a strong strength of will.

This next excerpt was taken from *The Hunger Games* by Suzanne Collins, where Katniss describes Peeta…

Medium height, stocky build, ashy blond hair that falls in waves over his forehead.

***

This excerpt is taken from my novella, THIRSTY…

Siobhan's glossy black hair rested on her slender shoulders, and the strands had blue and purple highlights, shiny as a raven's wing.

***

Think of it this way…hair is just another form of expression for most people. Especially with teens. For instance, if you're writing a young adult novel, make sure you do some research on current trends and hair colors so readers can relate and identify with your characters. Or if your story is about a snobby, affluent family, try adding descriptive words about their flawlessly coiffed hairstyles. Or if your novel includes a gang of teenaged bullies, include something about their long, greasy manes. You don't have to be cliché, but some stereotyping does help.

Here are some examples I wrote to show writers how to powerfully depict a character…

SHALLOW: I thought Angie's curly, long brunette hair was much prettier than my limp, dull brown hair that often looked frizzy.

SHOWING: Compared to Angie's thick, chocolate curls, my own mousy brown hair hung in limp frizzy strands.

Please compare the following two examples…

SHALLOW: She was a curvaceous girl with light brown skin, and she had long hair that was a brownish color.

SHOWING: She wore her buxom beauty with pride. Her caramel skin appeared flawless and the tumbling locks of her rich brown hair fell over one shoulder.

Notice the differences between the shallow description and the more vivid "showing" one?

Here's one more example taken from the young adult novel, *Jessica's Guide to Dating on the dark Side* by Beth Fantaskey. Please study this example…

Lucius Vladescu's longish glossy black hair was out of place in Lebanon County, Pennsylvania, but he would have fit right in with the European models in *Cosmopolitan* magazines.

***

Those examples should help writers to skillfully describe the characters in their own stories.

HAIR COLOR

This chapter should give writers inspiration for describing their character's hair color. Not only can a character's facial features tell the reader a thing or two about them, but their hair color can also reveal things about the characters in your fictional world.

One way to vividly describe a character's hair color is to be creative and not use boring descriptive words. Natural hair color is usually black, blonde, brown, gray, or red.

Please read these examples I wrote to illustrate how to describe a character's hair...

SHALLOW: Mary had short, blonde hair.

SHOWING: Mary's shorn brassy locks cupped her oval face.

SHALLOW: She had copper tones in her long hair.

SHOWING: The glowing sunset highlighted the glossy copper tones of her long hair.

SHALLOW: She had wispy dark colored hair.

SHOWING: A strand of dark, wispy hair tumbled across her forehead.

SHALLOW: The slender girl had thick reddish curls.

SHOWING: Soft, reddish ringlets bounced off her slim shoulders.

SHALLOW: He had light-colored hair that looked dirty and greasy.

SHOWING: His flaxen mane hung slack, caked with soot and sweat.

Notice the differences between the shallow description and the more vivid "showing" one?

This list should give writers some creative and original ideas for their own unique character descriptions.

List of vivid hair colors:

Highlights (blond, gold, black, red, auburn, etc.)

Arctic blond

Ash Brown

Ash-Blond

Auburn

Beige White

Black

Blonde

Brunette

Burgundy

Buttermilk

Butterscotch

Caramel

Chardonnay

Chestnut

Chocolate

Cinnamon

Copper

Coppery Red

Dark

Dirty blonde

Domino

Ebony

Fair

Fiery

Flame Red

Flaxen

Ginger

Golden

Gray

Honey

Honey Blonde

Irish Red

Jet black

Onyx

Pale Blonde

Pale Golden Blonde

Pecan

Raven

Red

Russet

Salt and Pepper

Wine-Red

Wheat

Highlights

Sable

Tawny

The information in this chapter should help writers to be original and creative when describing a character's appearance.

HAIR TYPES

This chapter covers different hair types that encompass all racial and ethnic races that writers can use to describe a character's flowing mane. Instead of just stating that a character's hair looked wavy or straight or curly, I suggest that writers be more inventive with their depictions.

Human hair has diverse types and textures. Hairstyles differ extensively across various cultures, and it is often used to signify a person's (character) social status or personality, and it can can convey their age, gender, ethnic background (race), or religion.

According to most cosmetologists (*I used to be one!*) there are three types of hair:

* African

* Asian

* Caucasian (European)

African-Americans usually have tight curls, very thick hair, and the color is a natural dark brown or black.

Asian hair is usually very straight and thick and shiny. It contrasts in colors from deep black to medium brown.

Caucasian or European hair can be straight, wavy, or curly. It fluctuates in color from very dark brown to flaxen. This hair type can be either fine, medium, or coarse.

Please compare these descriptive examples…

SHALLOW: She had short curly hair that was the color of blond.

SHOWING: She shook her blond head, the coiled strands resting on her shoulders.

SHALLOW: The woman had dark hair styled in a long braid.

SHOWING: The woman's ebony tresses fell down her back in a thick braid.

SHALLOW: The man had black hair cut into a bowl-shape.

SHOWING: His hair sat on his head like a dark bowl turned upside down.

SHALLOW: My long, wavy hair was styled into a ponytail.

SHOWING: I slicked my long, wavy hair into a stylish ponytail.

Notice the differences between the shallow description and the more vivid "showing" one?

Make sure that the hair descriptors you choose fit the character and their ethnic background.

List of descriptions to describe hair texture:

Bald patches

Balding

Bleached

Dry

Limp

Oily

Fine

Course

Straight

Corkscrew Curls

Curly

Nappy

Wavy

Thin / Fine

Frizzy

Thick

Wooly

Greasy

Brittle

Chemically damaged

Dandruff

Frizzy

Greasy

Hair loss / horseshoe

Ringlets / Spirals

Bouncy

Wispy

Stringy / Straggly

Tangled / Windblown

***

This chapter should inspire writers to become more creative when describing a character's hair for their readers.

HAIRSTYLES

A character's hairstyle will convey a lot about their personality. Most of us believe that we should *never* judge a book by its cover. But we all still do it on some sub-conscience level. The cover is what usually first attracts the eye, makes us curious, so we want to find out more…

But is it okay to judge a character by their hair?

A character's description is like first meeting someone and assessing their lifestyle, personality, and ethnic background. A feisty redhead might be from Ireland or a tall dark-skinned man wearing a turban might be from India.

Hairstyles from wild to conventional or trendy and chic, tells the reader a lot about their social class and personality. For instance, a former beauty pageant queen who visits the salon every Saturday morning to get her hair styled might be considered a narcissistic diva.

Or a dude who only goes to the barber every six months to get a haircut might be considered less concerned about his appearance. He might even be a slacker that's too cheap to waste money on his appearance.

Or maybe your character's a natural beauty that does their own hair at home. This type of character would be a DIY type. One who never wants to pay full price for anything, including a hairstylist.

Here are some examples I created to illustrate how to describe hairstyles…

SHALLOW: She had a puffy hairstyle.

SHOWING: Her hair stuck up like she'd been electrocuted.

SHALLOW: He had his hair cut into a spiky mohawk.

SHOWING: Thick spikes stood out from his scalp like a rooster.

Notice the differences between the shallow description and the more vivid "showing" one?

Get to know your characters by answering these questions:

For instance, how long does their character spend on their hair each morning?

How often do they change their hairstyle?

Does the character color their hair?

What is the length of their hair?

Are the characters a DIY type or a Salon diva?

What's their bad hair day solution?

How important is their hair on a scale from 1-10?

If the character has a shoulder-length, wash-and-go style, they might be a no-nonsense type personality. Or if the character has super short hair, then it most likely means they don't want to fuss over things in life, including their hair because they're sporty or outdoorsy. And characters with longer hairstyles might be more concerned with their looks.

These next illustration was taken from my novel, *Moonlight Mayhem*, to give writers an idea on how to describe a character's hair…

My ex stood at the counter with his friend and ordered a pizza. His hair tapered in the back and across both sides, but left heavy on top was styled into a spiky mess.

***

Here's another hairstyle example from my novel, *Lost in Starlight*…

Hayden turns his head and his light brown fauxhawk falls over his forehead in a messy yet somehow deliberate way, landing over his one strikingly blue eye. The other one is green. Besides the rare heterochromia iridis, he seems to be just another smokin' hot brainiac.

I add to my notes: *Weird eye color and member of the Amazing Hair Club.* Check.

***

List of words to describe hair texture:

Blow-dry

Braided

Classic Bob

Crown Braids

Curly

Elegant updo

Short and Spiky

Fringe

Pompadour

Blunt

Bangs

Wavy

Wedding Hair

Ponytail

Afro

Bangs

Beehive

Bouffant

Braided

Ballerina-Bun

Buzzed

Chignon

Comb-Over

Cornrows

Crew Cut

Dreadlocks

Fauxhawk / Mohawk

Finger-waves

Flattop

Fade

Spikes

Feathered

Mullet

Hair Descriptors

Bobbed

Bushy

Close-Cropped

Crinkly

Curtained

Damp

Dark

Disheveled / Tangled / Matted / Messy / Scraggly / Tousled

Flowing

Flyaway

Frizzy

Glossy

Greasy / Oily / Unwashed

Healthy-Looking

Loose

Luxuriant

Medium-Length

Moonlight-Pale

Natural

Ruffled

Shiny

Short

Shoulder-Length

Silky

Sleek

Slicked

Spiky

Straight

Thick

Thin

Thinning

Wavy

Well-Kept

Wind-Blown / Windswept

***

That list and the information provided in this chapter should help writers to be more imaginative when describing a character's outward appearance.

CLOTHING DESCRIPTION

Quote: "You can quickly convey a number of things about your characters based on the clothing they wear. You can also subvert the initial impression of your readers and your other characters. For example, think about a wealthy person and how that person might dress. You may have imagined a man in an expensive suit or a woman in designer clothes. You can immediately signal to your reader that a character is wealthy with markers such as these." —*author, Bridget McNulty*

Ah, fashion...one of my favorite subjects! But alas, since I started writing full-time and working from home, I mainly live in my sweat pants and pajamas. *So what does that say about me?* That I like to be comfortable while I'm writing and editing, or designing book covers. But when I go out, I do like to dress stylish and trendy.

This chapter will cover clothing descriptions, but mainly focusing on modern garments for both male and female characters.

Describing a character's wardrobe might seem tedious or unneeded, but consider this, clothing reveals a lot about the characters just as it does on actual people. Even if you're not writing about a fashionista, it's still good to know your character's personal style, which says a lot about who they are, such as personality, social status, age, profession, and even psychology.

Don't just emphasis the obvious features of a character's appearance, such as their eyes or height or weight, but also describe the type of clothes he/she wears.

Our clothing choices are often an expression of our distinct spirit and individuality, so characters should dress to match their own unique personalities, too.

Below is an excerpt from one of my novels, *Shattered Silence* to illustrate how to describe a character's clothing and personality…

He shrugged off a worn leather jacket and draped it over an armchair, displaying a long-sleeved black shirt. The guy was the epitome of hip. With artfully mussed hair, low-slung jeans, motorcycle boots, and model good looks, just a glimpse of Trent Donovan caused female hormones to rage, teenage girls to swoon, and mouths to drool.

***

Clothing descriptions can be a powerful and effective visual for the reader. It can say a lot about your character's personality without having to "tell" the reader about their likes, dislikes, or background. This is especially helpful if you write in the young adult or new adult genres. Most teens like to express themselves and their individuality though fashion.

I admit I enjoy writing description.

Does that mean that I always craft it correctly?

No. Sometimes I do an info-dump, and then I have to go back and figure out a clever way to lace it into the narrative.

Here's an excerpt taken from *All Lined Up* by Cora Carmack that nicely conveys a character's description. Please examine this example...

Down in the yard, highlighted by one of the floodlights affixed to the outside of the house, is another gorgeous guy wearing dark, worn jeans, scuffed boots, and a smirk that oscillates between infuriating and adorable. He's got dark hair and a delectable touch of scruff along his jaw, and he looks entirely entertained by my mental breakdown.

***

Here is a list that should help writers with clothing descriptions. In case writers aren't up-to-date on fashion terms, this terminology should be used a general reference.

List of clothing styles and types:

Preppy: Plaid Skirts, Sweater Vests, Pearl Necklaces

Punk: Skinny Jeans, Leather, Studs, Piercings

Modest: Covered Up, Long Skirts, Sweaters

Sophisticated: Suits, Trousers, Pencil Skirts, Blouses

Sporty: Sweats, T-Shirts, Tennis Shoes, Sneakers, and Board-Shorts

Edgy: Converse, Skinny Jeans, Black Boots, Basically Some Punk but Not All Punk

Vintage: Older Styles, Like an Old Band on Your T-Shirt

Western: Brown Leather, Blue, Browns, And Orange: Cowboy Boots

Nautical/Preppy: Blue Red and White, Bows, and Collars

Summer Attire: Sandals, Loose Sundress, Sandals, Flats, Floppy Hats

Futuristic: Metallic, What You Imagine People In The Future to Wear

Rocker/Emo: Band Logos, Kind of Punk, Skinny Jeans, Leather-Studded Belts

Boho-Chic: Layered Clothing, Baggy Shirts, Big Purses, Long Necklaces, Lots of Jewelry

Flirty: Low-Cut Dress, Mini-Skirt, Stilettos

Casual: Shorts, Pants, Tennis Shoes, Flip-Flops, Etc.

Formal: Floor-Length Gowns, Tuxedo, High-Heels, Wingtip Shoes

Casual Chic: Designer Jeans, T-Shirts, Sneakers, Khaki Pants, Capris, and Flowing Dresses

Hippie: Baggy Clothes, Peace Signs, Long Skirts, Bell-Bottoms, Tie-Dye

Punk/Emo: Skinny Jeans; Short Skirts; Flats; Converses; Graphic T-Shirts

Prep: Ripped Jeans; Dark Wash Denim; Babydoll Blouses; Flip-Flops; Big White Sunglasses

Dressy: Button-Down Shirts; Strappy Heels; Big Bags; Vests; Shirt Dress; Straight Legged Pants

Hip-Hop: Shoes-Forces, Dunks, High Tops; Baggy Jeans and Oversized Shirts

Beach/Boho: Big Shades; Headbands; Sundresses; Khaki Shorts; Tank-Tops

***

This next scene (condensed) was taken from my book, *Reckless Revenge* to demonstrate how you can weave in action, emotion, humor, and intensity to illustrate how to describe a character's clothing and appearance...

Stalker Boy looked about eighteen or nineteen, but not much older. Maybe he was a transfer student repeating a grade. He had his arms crossed and one leg bent at the knee, his booted heel planted on the wall. His shoulder-length black hair made him look like an ancient warrior, and his long bangs fell forward to conceal one eye. When he turned his attention to the teachers standing awkwardly near the podium, I took the opportunity to study him. His skin appeared completely unmarred, with pronounced cheekbones and a strong jawline. He was tall, much taller than me, but I was only 5'6. While

I stared at him, only for a moment, the air seemed to glow around his body in warm currents of incandescent sunbeams, almost like an aura.

***

How did this description of the character make you feel?

Did you get a very detailed and vivid image of him?

Did you get an inkling of his personality or background?

This chapter and the examples provided should really help writers to portray characters as real people and turn scenes into fresh and vivid prose.

CHARACTER GARMENTS

There are many different ways to describe places, objects, and characters. Descriptive writing that effectively uses sensory details will allow the reader to do more than merely "see" the words, but experience the story. One way to do that is to describe a character's wardrobe.

Writers should have fun when illustrating a character's apparel, but don't waste too much description on any minor or secondary characters. Too much description can disrupt the pace, in addition to making the reader assume that these characters are more important than they actually are to the storyline.

Please examine these examples…

SHALLOW: Harry was a thin man who always wore a tweed suit.

SHOWING: Harry's tweed suit hung shabbily off his lanky frame.

Notice the differences between the shallow description and the more vivid "showing" one?

Here are two excerpts from my novel, *Smash Into You*. The first one describes a group of college kids in the cafeteria.

Please examine this example...

The scent of *Eau de School*, a mixture of fried foods and mingled fragrances overwhelmed my senses. We shuffled forward with our trays, and I took in the room with its dull beige walls and crowded tables. A couple of students donned pajamas with various degrees of bedhead and five students in trendy clubbing attire seemed hung over, but the majority of people wore normal college garb: jeans, shorts, and wrinkled T-shirts.

This second excerpt describes a girl at the heroine's college. Please examine this example...

Brooklyn turned on her iPad. On her ears were diamond studs, flashing in the sunlight. She gave off this effortlessly street-chic vibe dressed in a stylish knit pullover with tight black jeans, leather knee-high boots, and a crocheted beanie that all screamed *money*. But I supposed having your face plastered on billboards and gracing magazine covers paid well. In contrast, Jade and Claire weren't excessively beautiful like Brooklyn.

***

List to describe fabrics:

Plaid

Tweed

Color Block

Ponte Knit

Box Pleat

Chiffon

Jersey

Crepe

Linen

Silk

Tweed

Velour

Leather

Suede

Polka Dot

Embroidered

Floral

***

Here is another longer excerpt taken from my book, *Beautifully Broken* to give writers an idea on how to describe a first-person character's clothing...

My stomach lurched when I spotted Brittany Witheridge and the dreaded *Trendies* ascending the steps of the school. The Trendies included Brittany's best friend Kayla Bishop, and their other two friends, Heather Keyes and Emily Cast.

Brittany had straight hair the color of blackberries, which flowed around her like spun silk brushing her shoulders and highlighting her tan skin. In her slim jeans, she was svelte, with super long legs and minimal curves. She had the same slightly opaque brown eyes and distinct Asian features as her proud Chinese mother.

Kayla, tossing her blond locks over her shoulder, hurried on her short, fake-tanned legs to catch up with Brittany's longer strides as they entered the building, joining the throng of urban yuppie students that dominated the school.

I yanked the hood over my head, wishing I'd chosen something else to wear other than frayed jeans, a cropped pink tee that showed off my sparkly bellyring, black hoodie, and my kickass Doc Martens ankle-boots. Not like I was rebelling. I like to think I had my own quirky sense of style.

***

After reading this, what is your impression of these characters?

Are they wealthy or underprivileged? Stuck up or nice?

Does each girl have a distinct style and what does it say about them?

What insight did you gleam by their appearances?

Did you imagine their history and background, too?

I assume that you've formed immediate opinions about these teenage girls through this short description, which is what I intended.

I have included a help list of descriptive words that writers can use as a handy reference whenever describing their characters garments.

List of words to describe clothing:

Active

Adjustable

Adorable

Affordable

Asymmetrical

Banded

Beaded

Big & tall

Bloused

Boho Chic

Bold

Bootcut

Boxy

Breathable

Busty

Button-Down

Chic

Classic

Collared

Comfortable

Comfy

Contemporary

Couture

Cross-Stitched

Cushioned

Custom

Cutting-Edge

Dapper

Designer

Discounted

Distressed

Double-Breasted

Durable

Eco-Friendly

Edgy

Efficient

Everyday

Fabric-Lined

Fashionable

Faux

Feminine

Fitted

Flexible

Form-Fitting

Funky

Glitzy

Gypsy

Hand-Sewn

Hand-Washed

High-Waisted

Imported

Innovative

Intricate

Jagged

Knee-Length

Knit

Lacy

Lightweight

Lined

Loose

Metallic

Mini-Shirt

Minimalist

Modern

Old-Fashioned

Opaque

Open-Backed

Organic

Oversized

Patchwork

Patterned

Peasant

Petite

Pleated

Plunging

Practical

Pragmatic

Preppy

Pressed

Printed

Professional

Push-Up Bra

Quilted

Racerback

Reinforced

Relaxed

Retro

Retro Print

Ribbed

Rocker-Style

Romantic

Rugged

Scooped-Neck

See-Through

Semi-Formal

Sheer

Short-Sleeve

Silky

Simple

Skinny-Fit

Sleek

Slinky

Slip-On

Slouchy

Snug

Sophisticated

Sporty

Stitched

Strapless

Strappy

Stretchy

Stylish

Tailored

Textured

Tight

Timeless

Trendy

Tunic Length

Leather

Versatile

Vintage

Water-Resistant / Waterproof

***

That concludes my advice on clothing descriptions. In the next several chapters, I'll discuss how to incorporate sensory details into your settings, which will give your readers a vibrant image of the locations within your amazing fictional world.

THE SENSES

Quote: "A common writing fault and often difficult to recognize, although once the principle is grasped, cutting away filters is an easy means to more vivid writing." —*Janet Burroway, Writing Fiction*

World-building is a critical and necessary part of any work of fiction. Vivid descriptions almost always use specific, concrete details so the reader can "visualize" what is being described or experienced by the characters through one or more of five senses.

To describe vivid characters and settings, writers should use the Deep POV technique by involving all of the senses in their descriptions. Remember that "telling" a reader what a character is seeing, hearing, touching, or tasting is *not* using Deep POV.

Powerful descriptive writing should always strive to involve the use of every human sense. It is also a great way of making all of your scenes more three-dimensional. In order to do this, I think it's important to stay in Deep POV to construct a more realistic and engaging scene.

There are many ways to achieve a Deeper POV, but here are a few sure-fire ways to enhance your prose.

The main five senses are:

Sight: What your character sees. (Describe images and the setting through their eyes.) The glint of sunlight on a stained glass window or the shiny black wings of a raven.

Hear: Noises that surround your character(s) in every scene. A dog howling or an old furnace grumbling.

Smell: Make clear the scents, aromas, and odors. The scent of fresh laundry or the aroma of orange blossoms.

Touch: Describe the feel and texture of their surroundings. Show the feel of icy snow or the luxurious touch of silk sheets.

Taste: Depict the tastes of your character's world. The tart flavor of a lime or the harsh burn and acrid taste of whiskey.

*** *

When describing the setting writers should take into consideration the different sensory elements within each scene. Writers should illustrate the scenery for readers by using some of the five senses.

For instance, a writer should describe the coldness of the bathroom floor, the interlacing stench of perspiration and the flowery scent of deodorant of a gym locker-room, or the sweet aroma of a rose garden.

Here are a few ways to make your scenes more vivid for the reader…

Be specific

How often have you gotten a comment from an editor or critique partner asking you to be more specific? Do beta-readers think that your writing seems a bit vague?

If writers are more accurate in their descriptions, it will be effortless for the reader to imagine your world.

Don't just state there was a car, but he drove a BMW. It's not a hat, but a Nike baseball cap, etc.

Don't just state it was a street, but describe it as a gravel road, or cracked asphalt, etc.

Don't state that there was a big house, but a colossal mansion dominated the estate, etc.

Do research

For settings based on actual locations, the Internet is one of the easiest places to do a bit of quick and easy research. For instance, a search online for "Houston, Texas" will bring up numerous websites that provide travel information, facts, and the state's history, which can enhance the storyline.

Or use Google Maps to get a sense of the location, or do an image search and browse photos. And a writer can watch videos on YouTube.

Read a book on the history of a city or town. Also, if writers looked up words, such as "Texas vacation" or "travel journal" they should gain a wealth of knowledge about a place through reading personal accounts of a trip.

Of course, if you're writing a historical novel, a lot more detailed research might be needed to avoid inaccuracies.

Use sensory details

If writers include sensory details experienced by the narrator, the reader will be able to clearly envision colors, shapes, temperatures, odors, and even the feel of textures.

Distinctive words

Only use adjectives that are unique, and steer clear of ambiguous adjectives that label an object or describe a location. A specific verb or noun will anchor any description in a more effective way. Explanatory labels are words, such as *pretty, mature, amazing, significant,* or *incredible.* Instead use descriptive adjectives, such as *doe-eyed, frizzy, rough, tattered, greasy,* or *overgrown.*

Be detailed, yet have fun with your descriptions!

In the next several chapters, I go over in more detail ways to incorporate all of the five senses into your own writing.

SIGHT

"Sight" is one of the main senses that a character would use to describe a place or another character. Whenever a writer states that a character "saw something" or "looked at something" when describing their surroundings, like a place (setting) or an object, use the sense of sight to vividly describe it by mentioning the colors, shapes, and images.

Optical details that appeal to the sense of *sight* can ensure that the reader is able to imagine characters, and add tangible specifics to a setting. For instance, a room can become more than just a vacant, ambiguous receptacle. Through the characters "eyes," it becomes a dynamic, rectangle-shaped room with dark wood paneling and a stained hardwood floor. A graphic description allows readers to place themselves *within* the scene.

Always strive to revise filter words like *see / saw / could see* when describing a setting, character, or item. Also, writers should avoid using "looked" or "appeared" to describe an object, setting or character expression because it is considered filtering (shallow writing). Alternatives could be: *viewed, regarded, observed, spotted, glimpsed,* or *catch sight of,* etc.

Including sensory details like "sight" to the narrative will help the reader to vividly imagine the character's surroundings, such as these:

The sun rising in the distant cast golden beams over the heads of the houses.

Her lush locks of hair had a silky, black gloss.

The autumn leaves littering the ground were a burst of orange, brown, and red hues.

The vampire's pale skin gleamed in the moonlight and his blood-flecked eyes narrowed on my neck.

The shimmery light of the moon created a soft glow above the trees.

The sun glinted in the blue sky like a sovereign of shiny gold.

***

The objective of Deep POV is to secure the reader inside the character's head without using shallower words that litter your prose and distance your reader.

Here are some examples I created to illustrate how to use this *sense* in your own stories…

SHALLOW: I could see Malcolm walking toward me.

SHOWING: Malcolm strode toward me with a brisk gait.

SHALLOW: I looked at the forest.

SHOWING: The forest was a vast landscape of greenery.

SHALLOW: He <u>saw</u> a raccoon walk across the road.

SHOWING: A raccoon ambled across the narrow road.

SHALLOW: The house <u>looked</u> quiet and peaceful.

SHOWING: The house was too quiet, and almost peaceful.

SHALLOW: I <u>see</u> the moon lift overhead.

SHOWING: The moon hung in an inky sky overhead.

***

Here are two different scenes to review. The first is written in a *telling* style (weak visual). The telling scene does convey the facts and details, but it does so in a flavorless and nondescript way with too many filter words. (I have underlined what I consider to be shallower writing.)

Please compare these descriptive examples…

SHALLOW:

Matt <u>saw</u> a young boy in the bushes. His skin and clothes <u>appeared</u> filthy and his hair was unkempt. Matt <u>saw</u> snot dripping from his nose. The boy's <u>expression communicated</u> to Matt that <u>there was</u> something he was <u>sad</u> about. Next, he <u>noticed</u> a leather dog collar held in the boy's hand, but no dog. Then Matt <u>knew</u> something was very wrong indeed as he <u>looked around</u> the park.

SHOWING:

Matt almost stumbled over a young boy crouched in the bushes. His skin was filthy, with dried mud stuck to his cheek, and his shirt and jeans covered in grass stains. The boy glanced up through his scruffy hair with bloodshot eyes rimmed with tears. A big gob of snot dripped from his nose. Matt squatted near the kid and his gaze caught a leather dog collar clutched in the boy's fist. He scanned the park. No sign of the lost dog.

***

List of alternatives to describing the sense of sight:

Angular / Rangy / Gaunt

Dull / Cloudy / Gloomy

Hideous / Nauseating / Vile

Splintered / Cracked / Fractured

Ashen / Pale / Insipid

Dusty / Grimy / Grubby

Gargantuan / Immense / Immeasurable

Pocked / Dented / Blemished

Spongy / Malleable / Soggy

Elegant / Stylish / Classy

Pointed / Sharp / Jagged

Spotted / Speckled / Patterned

Feathery / Downy / Fluffy

Jutting / Protruding / Overhanging

Boiling / Fiery / Burning

Prickly / Spiny / Sharp

Steamy / Humid / Sweltering

Knobbed / Knotted / Twisted

Pulpy / Mushy / Soft

Stubbly / Bristly / Bearded

Rocky / Bumpy / Stony

Bubbling / Effervescing / Simmering

Swollen / Bulky / Husky

Flushed / Blushing / Rosy

Lean / Wiry / Sinewy

Ruffled / Tousled / Rumpled

Foggy / Muddled / Hazy

Dense / Impenetrable / Opaque

Furry / Shaggy / Hirsute

Tidy / Clean / Polished

Flawless / Immaculate / Spotless

Fuzzy / Nebulous / Shadowy

Lopsided / Uneven / Irregular

Translucent / Transparent / Clear

Cluttered / Chaotic / Strewed

Shimmering / Iridescent / Glistening

***

That list should inspire writers to be more creative when describing a scene. As you revise, please keep in mind that visual details encourage the reader to create a vivid mental image of the characters and setting in their mind.

SOUND

"Hearing" is one of the most common senses to use in description. Whenever your character hears a noise or the scene changes to a new location, the sense of hearing should be applied for a Deeper POV while depicting the scene. Writers should use the sense of "hearing" to provide the reader with more sensory details.

The sense of *hearing* is an important means of communication for your characters. Next to visual details like *sight*, auditory sensations should be included in every genre, no matter where or when your imaginary story takes place. This is because sounds will give the reader an essential experience of the fictional world and often remind them of personal experiences, while creating a dramatic images in their minds.

Common filter words are *heard / hear / could hear* that can create narrative distance. And if your reader already knows in whose POV the scene is written, then why would you need to explain what he/she is hearing?

Also, the sense of hearing can be a powerful trigger for your characters. While writing a descriptive setting, consider the memories that music can produce, or the sound of a lover's voice, or the jangle of the ice cream truck when you were a child. Certain loud sounds can make a person wince or tense up, while other softer noises can make us loosen up and smile. A scene that includes the sense of hearing and sounds is much more likely to induce an emotional reaction in the reader. In my opinion, the word sound is extensively overused in fiction.

Including details of sounds will help the reader to strongly envision the character's surroundings, such as these:

The haunting caw of a crow flying over a wheat field.

The wailing of a fussy baby.

The shriek of a firetruck's siren as the vehicle lumbers down the street.

The sizzling of bacon frying in a pan.

The soft tempo of rain pattering against a windowpane.

Writers should also eradicate any filter references, such as *sounds / sound* from their writing that "tell" instead of "show." Alternatives could be: *noise, hum, echo, thud, reverberation, crash, jingle, clatter,* or *vibration.* Any of which are more specific for the reader.

Here are some examples I created to illustrate how to use this *sense* in your own stories…

SHALLOW: I <u>heard</u> ghostly moans coming from within the haunted house.

SHOWING: Ghostly moans came from within the haunted house.

SHALLOW: Kate <u>heard</u> the distant <u>sound</u> of a train.

SHOWING: The train's piercing whistle sliced the air.

SHALLOW: I <u>could hear</u> the bushes shake with the <u>sounds</u> of a snake.

SHOWING: The bushes quaked with the distinct jangle of a rattle snake.

SHALLOW: He <u>hears</u> a yowling <u>sound</u> coming from the dark bedroom.

SHOWING: A yowling seeps from beneath the closed bedroom door.

SHALLOW: She <u>heard</u> the <u>sound</u> of the car coming.

SHOWING: The Ford's tires screeched, kicking up gravel on the road.

***

Not all filter words can be completely removed from your prose because that would be difficult, so if using a filter word like "sound" in the sentence creates easier readability and avoids passive writing, then I would leave it. (I also think it's okay to use when describing a tone of voice in dialogue.)

Here are two longer scenes. The first one is shallow with too many filtering references. (I have underlined what I consider to be shallower writing.)

Please compare these descriptive examples…

SHALLOW:

As he went inside the old house on Clover Lane, Jake heard a leaky faucet. The sound was eerie. When he moved through the rooms, the sound of his boots on the hardwood floor made a loud echo. Then Jake heard a growling sound and he felt afraid.

Was something else in the house?

Feeling scared out of his wits (cliché), Jake froze in fear (cliché). The sound of a barking dog made him flinch. He turned to look around and he saw a big dog in the doorway. He heard the animal panting loudly. Jake was fearful so he left the house.

SHOWING:

Jake snuck into the old house on Clover Lane. The eerie *drip, drip, drip* from a leaky faucet signaled that it came from the kitchen. As he explored the cobwebbed space, his boots echoed on the hardwood floor.

Just as he entered a bedroom, a low growl resonated throughout the lower rooms. He wasn't alone. His pulse pounded. A dog loudly barked from somewhere inside the residence, and the menacing threat made him flinch.

Jake slowly turned to scan the room, and spotted a beady-eyed bulldog hulking in the doorway. The dog's tongue hung out of its mouth, panting noisily. With his legs shaking, Jake backed up and left the house.

***

List of words to describe sound:

Banging

Cracking

Hushing

Rapping

Snarling

Barking

Crashing

Jangling

Rasping

Snoring

Bawling

Croaking

Jingling

Rattling

Stuttering

Belching

Crunching

Ringing

Tapping

Blaring

Crying

Moaning

Ripping / Tearing

Booming

Dripping

Rumbling

Tinkling

Burping

Exploding

Mumbling

Rustling

Thudding / Thumping

Buzzing

Fizzing

Scratching /Scraping

Chattering

Gagging

Ticking

Chiming

Gasping

Noisy

Screeching

Twittering

Chirping

Warbling

Clanging

Grating

Piercing

Wheezing

Clapping

Growling

Pinging

Clicking

Grunting

Plopping / Popping

Clinking

Gurgling

Splashing

Cooing

Hissing

Quacking

Squawking

Whizzing

Coughing

Honking

Snapping

Whooping

***

The addition of auditory awareness gives the writer the opportunity to create a more detailed, layered, and textured scene.

SMELL

This chapter discusses how to revise filter words from your sentences by using the five senses and omitting the filtering words *smell / smelled* from your prose to avoid narrative distance. However, it is *always* okay to use filter words in dialogue.

The sense of smell is generally neglected in fiction writing. However, it is the sense of smell that is most intimately linked to the brain. The receptors in the brain that are responsible for processing odors are also close to the area that's in charge of memory storage. Because of this link, smells are able to trigger intense memories. And the sense of smell has an especially strong influence over our moods, reactions, and emotions.

The awareness of "smells" can be a fun way to add a layer of complexity and realism to your descriptions. And smell is a natural reaction that can be included in almost every scene that you write. The human sense of *smell* has the extraordinary ability to evoke a strong response in readers by producing a memory or emotional reaction, such as the scent of a woman's perfume, the aroma of freshly brewed coffee, or the stink of rotting garbage.

Smell can help a character to appreciate the aroma of a home-cooked meal, the whiff of freshly washed hair, or the scent of spring flowers. But it can also be a warning system, notifying a character to certain dangers, like smoke, rotten food, or dangerous chemicals.

The sense of smell can affect the setting, and create a strong response for both the reader and the characters. Smell incites sensory details that will help the reader to strongly envision the character's surroundings, such as these:

The lingering aroma of cut grass.

The mouthwatering scent of freshly baked cookies.

The offending stench of body odor.

The whiff of pine from a Christmas tree.

The stinky gas fumes of an urban city.

Common filter words are *smell / smelled / smelling / could smell* that can create narrative distance.

Here are some examples I created to illustrate how to use this *sense* in your own stories…

SHALLOW: Lori could <u>smell</u> the tree scents in the air.

SHOWING: Aromas drifted from the meadow—pine and cedar—as a strong gust blew across the rippling lake.

SHALLOW: I <u>smelled</u> the chicken burning on the stove.

SHOWING: A burning odor wafted from the stove.

SHALLOW: He <u>could smell</u> her strong cologne from across the room.

SHOWING: Her potent perfume roamed across the room.

SHALLOW: Lori <u>smelled</u> something gross.

SHOWING: Lori wrinkled her nose at the offending stench.

SHALLOW: A thick sulfur <u>smell</u> was filling one corner of the gym.

SHOWING: A thick sulfur odor filled one corner of the gym.

Here are two longer scenes. The first one is shallow with too many filtering references. (I have underlined what I consider to be shallower writing.)

Please compare these descriptive examples…

SHALLOW:

I <u>smelled</u> something smoky. Then I <u>saw</u> the fire rise in the next room of my house. I <u>watched</u> the flames quickly <u>began to</u> burn the furniture and drapes. I <u>smelled</u> smoke and <u>noticed</u> it fill the air. Then I <u>heard</u> the fire alarm start to ring really loudly. The <u>smell</u> of burning wood made my eyes water.

I <u>saw</u> the open windows <u>began to</u> release a dark, thick smoke that <u>smelled</u> terrible. I <u>felt</u> myself choking because it was hard to breathe. I <u>smelled</u> melting paint and scorched timber. I <u>knew</u> I had to get out of the house before it burned to the ground.

SHOWING:

The pungent scent of smoke wafted throughout the house like deadly incense.

The next room resembled a wall of flames that quickly devoured the furniture and long drapes. Billows of smoke filled the air and triggered the fire alarm, which yowled like a dying animal. Blinking, I rubbed my watery eyes, but my vision was still bleary.

A long cord of thick smoke leaked out the open windows like a withering snake.

Choking on the fumes, I staggered and tried to breathe. The stench of melting paint and scorched timber stung my nose. I had to escape before the house burned to the ground.

List of words to describe smells:

Anosmatic

Deodorizing

Halitosis

Inodorous

Anomic

Fresh

Heady

Muscatel

Osmic

Gamy

Hircine

Nasal

Deodorized

Grave lent

Indurate

Aroma

Aura

Balm

Fragrance

Incense

Odor

Redolence

Savor

Scent

Smelly

Spicy

Perfume

Bouquet

Pong

Whiff

Waft

Reek

Tang

Pong

Sniff

List for describing diverse smells:

Stinky

Stench

Acidy

Acrid

Antiseptic

Aromatic

Balmy

Biting

Bitter

Briny

Burnt

Citrusy

Comforting

Corky

Damp

Dank

Distinctive

Earthy

Fishy

Flowery

Fragrant

Fresh

Fruity

Gamy

Gaseous

Heavy

Lemony

Medicinal

Metallic

Mildewed

Minty

Moldy

Musky

Musty

Odorless

Peppery

Perfumed

Piney

Pungent

Putrid

Reek

Rose

Rotten

Savory

Scented

Sharp

Sickly

Skunky

Smoky

Sour

Spicy

Spoiled

Stagnant

Stench

Stinking

Sulphur

Sweaty

Sweet

Tart

Tempting

Vinegary

Woody

Yeasty

**

List of "smell/scent" adjectives:

Clean, delicious, fragrant, crisp, moist, juicy, breezy, refreshing, unpolluted, fresh, strong, sweet, perfume, fragrance, cologne, aftershave, toilet water, eau de toilette, body spray, aroma, hint, trace, whiff, bouquet, sniff, tinged, pungent, spicy, overpowering, smelly, reeking, fetid, malodorous, rank, putrid, noxious, medicinal, musty pungent, putrid, rancid acrid, antiseptic, bitter, burning, choking, rich, rotten, salty, smoky, sour, spicy, stale, stinky, odor, spoor, stench, reek, tang, pong, forceful, dank.

***

Anytime that you can remove the sensory "tell" from your scenes and clearly state whatever it is the character *saw* or *felt* or *tasted* or *heard* or *smelled*, it will automatically put you into Deeper POV. Just remember as you're revising your manuscript that the addition of olfactory details can help establish the mood of a scene by triggering the senses.

TOUCH

The human sense of *touch* can provoke a sensory response in the reader. It allows the reader to feel the softness of a warm, freshly washed towel, the abrasiveness of a brick wall, or the prickly stab of a cactus in bloom. It lets the reader sense the sharp, cold slap of winter winds on the hero's skin, the scorching blaze of a roaring fire in a hearth, or the itchy feel of an old wool blanket.

Texture describes the way something feels when touched with a character's hands, fingertips, or skin. I've noticed in the manuscripts I critique that the sense of "touch" is one the most unused descriptor by writers.

Dr. David Linden states that the human brain has evolved to have two distinct but parallel pathways for processing touch information. The first is a sensory pathway, which gives us the facts about touch, such as vibration, pressure, and fine texture. The second pathway processes social and emotional information, determining the emotional content of mostly interpersonal touch using different sensors in the skin. This pathway activates brain regions associated with social bonding, pleasure and pain centers.

The sense of touch can encourage a character to investigate the world around them by feeling objects and discovering the texture, shape, and size of things. Tangible images can be powerful sensory triggers if used correctly. They allow a reader not only to visualize a scene, but to experience it. Exclusion of the sense of touch in a scene prevents the reader from being deeply immersed in the story, and it can cause narrative distance.

To give readers a very clear and vivid image of the setting, writers should include the sense of touch to their narratives. It will help the reader to intensely imagine the character's surroundings, such as these:

My hand gripped the bottle of sticky syrup.

The Egyptian cotton sheets felt like lying on soft and luxurious cloud.

My fingertips burned when I gripped the steaming mug of coffee.

She sat on the freshly mowed grass, the spiky stalks pricking her bare skin.

When he grabbed a bag of ice from the freezer, the coldness made him shiver.

Writing with filter words, such as "I touched the cat's fur" or "It feels so soft" is almost never necessary in Deeper POV. Instead, simply describe the feeling of the object. Alternative words could be: *stroked, handled, sensed, experienced, caressed,* or *contacted,* etc. And while using the word "touch" or "touched" in a sentence isn't necessarily wrong, it does give the reader a weaker visual in my opinion.

Here are some examples I created to illustrate how to use this *sense* in your own stories…

SHALLOW: I felt cold when I stepped outside the warm house.

SHOWING: The chilly winds nipped at my cheeks and I shuddered.

SHALLOW: I felt the cat's soft fur coat.

SHOWING: I petted the cat's silky fur.

SHALLOW: I touched the shaggy carpet.

SHOWING: My fingers stroked the thick, shag carpeting.

SHALLOW: She felt the rough bark on the pine tree.

SHOWING: Her hand stroked the rough bark on the towering pine.

SHALLOW: The ocean waves felt cold on my bare skin.

SHOWING: The icy waves crashed onto the beach and soaked my skin.

***

In the shallow examples, I did not underline the shallower writing, but see if you can clearly identify it.

This list of textures and descriptors should be used as a vital reference when describing something the character touches or feels.

List of words to describe textures:

Abrasive / Ragged / Serrated / Notched

Blunt / Dull / Rounded / Unsharpened

Scarred / Scratched / Scraped / Grooved

Broken / Fragmented / Cracked / Indented / Dented /

Bubbly / Foamy / Soapy / Fizzy / Frothy

Soft / Mushy / Slushy / Squishy /

Bulging / Bulky / Massive / Hulking / Compact /

Bumpy / Lumpy / Ribbed / Ridged / Rutted

Crisp / Crunchy / Brittle / Crumbly / Brisk / Nippy

Bushy / Shaggy / Hairy / Luxuriant

Cold / Cool / Freezing / Frigid / Icy / Chilly / Chapped

Corrugated / Grooved / Uneven / Ridged

Wet / Damp / Clammy / Moist / Saturated / Slimy / Slippery / Sodden / Soggy

Spongy / Springy / Mushy

Dry / Dusty / Sooty / Wither / Dehydrate

Encrusted / Covered / Coated / Caked / Enveloped

Engraved / Etched / Imprinted / Inscribed / Carved

Fat / Thick / Solid / Firm / Hard / Crisp / Dense / Plump

Feathery / Fluffy / Fleecy / Cottony / Fuzzy / Furry

Flimsy / Gossamer / Smooth / Sheer / Silky / Filmy

Swollen / Bloated / Puffy / Inflated

Gelatinous / Jellylike / Sticky / Gooey / Tacky

Glassy / Glazed / Glossy / Slick

Granular / Grainy / Coarse / Rough / Gritty / Coarse / Sandy

Hot / warm / Scalding / Burning / Humid / steamy / sweltering

Leathery / Stringy / Fibrous / Gristly

Malleable / Rubbery / Flexible / Limp

Narrow / Thin / Slim / Threadlike / Frail / Fragile

Greasy / Grimy / Oily / Oleaginous / Fatty

Ornamented / Ornate / Flowery /

Sharp / Pointy / jagged / Razor-sharp / Prickly / Bristly / Itchy

Rusty / Corroded / Eroded /

Scored / Scraped / Scratched / Nicked

Spiky / Thorny / Barbed

Waxy

Plastic

Wooden

***

Most of us have heard the saying, "*show, don't tell*" many times. In order for a reader to become deeply involved in a story, they must be able to visualize the setting, hear the sounds, imagine touching the objects, and even smell everything within the scene.

This chapter should help writers to revise your own stories into great reads.

TASTE

Fiction writing that lacks any descriptions is in peril of becoming dull and uninteresting. Description can create a more concrete and sensory experience for our readers.

Sensory details like *taste* can be a great tool for writers in any genre.

It is important to remember as your revising your manuscript that humans first learn about the world around them through the five senses. They are a person's initial source of knowledge about our surroundings. Consequently, descriptive writing that encompasses vivid, sensory details like "taste" is more likely to engross the reader.

By including the human sense of taste, it allows a reader to do much more than simply read about whatever the character is tasting, such as food, the atmosphere, or air. Without the insertion of sensory details, the story might seem vague and generic.

The four common tastes are:

Sour / Salty / Bitter / Sweet

Synonyms for Taste:

Flavor (noun), delectability, deliciousness, flavor, goodness, pepperiness, saltiness, savoriness, sourness, spiciness, sweetness.

Meal (noun), banquet, barbecue, board, bread, consumption, cuisine, dinner, eating, fare, food, foodstuff, ingestion, meal, meat, morsel, nutriment, repast, spread, sustenance.

Propriety (noun), appropriateness, correctness, decorum, fittingness, manners, politeness, propriety, refinement, seemliness, suitability.

Eat (verb), bite, breakfast, consume, devour, dine, drink, eat, feast, feed, grub, gulp, ingest, lunch, picnic, snack, sip.

***

By directly engaging any of these taste sensations, a writer has the creative opportunity to involve a reader's senses.

To give readers a vivid picture of the setting, writers should include the sense of taste to their scenes. Sensory details such as this will help the reader to vividly imagine the character's surroundings, such as these:

The bitter sting of whiskey burned his throat.

The tanginess of the orange lingered on her tongue.

The crisp, salty potato chips made her thirsty.

The bubbly soda fizzed in her mouth.

I bit into a chocolate chip cookie, savoring the sugary flavor.

***

Below I have provided some examples of the wrong way to describe something a character tastes and the correct way through use of a Deeper POV to illustrate how to use this *sense* in your own stories. (In the shallow examples, I did not underline the shallower writing, but see if you can clearly identify it now that you're more aware of *showing* vs. *telling*.)

Please examine these sentences…

SHALLOW: The steak was burnt and tasted nasty.

SHOWING: He bit into the blackened piece of meat, but the steak had a charred flavor.

SHALLOW: The taste of stale bread made her want to spit it out.

SHOWING: The stale bread sat on her tongue and she had to force herself to swallow it.

SHALLOW: She liked the taste of grape juice.

SHOWING: She enjoyed the tangy flavor of grape juice.

SHALLOW: I ate an ice cream cone, because I liked the chocolate taste.

SHOWING: I licked the ice cream cone, the chocolate sweetness melting in my mouth.

SHALLOW: He kissed her, and tasted cherry chapstick.

SHOWING: He kissed her, and the flavor of her cherry chapstick made him smile.

***

This list of textures and tastes should be used as a vital reference when describing something the character eats or drinks.

List of words to describe how something tastes:

Acidic

Acrid

Bitter

Bland

Burnt

Buttery

Chalky

Cheesy

Chewy

Chocolaty

Citrusy

Creamy

Crispy

Crunchy

Doughy

Dry

Earthy

Fermented

Fiery / Hot

Fishy

Fizzy

Flakey

Flat

Flavorful

Fresh

Fried

Fruity

Gamey

Garlicky

Gelatinous

Glazed

Grainy

Greasy

Gooey

Gritty

Herbal

Cold / Icy

Juicy

Lemony

Malty

Mashed

Meaty

Mellow / Mild

Minty

Moist

Mushy

Nutty

Oily

Oniony

Overripe

Peppery

Pickled

Powdery

Raw

Refreshing

Ripe

Roasted

Robust

Salty

Sautéed

Savory

Seared

Seasoned

Sharp

Slimy

Smokey

Soggy

Soupy

Sour

Spicy

Spongy

Stale

Sticky

Stringy

Sugary or sweet

Sweet-and-sour

Syrupy

Tangy

Tart

Tasteless

Tender

Toasted

Tough

Unflavored

Unseasoned

Vinegary

Watery

Woody

Yeasty

Zesty

Zingy

List of adjectives to describe the sense of taste:

Amazing

Appealing

Appetizing

Delectable

Delicious

Delightful

Divine

Enjoyable

Excellent

Exquisite

Extraordinary

Fantastic

Finger Licking

Heavenly

Lip Smacking

Luscious

Marvelous

Mouthwatering

Palatable

Satisfying

Scrumptious

Superb

Tantalizing

Tasty

Terrific

Wonderful

Yummy

***

This chapter should really help give writers ideas on ways to include this sense in their narratives.

VIVID LOCATIONS

Quote: "Don't tell me the moon is shining; show me the glint of light on the broken glass." —*playwright and short story writer, Anton Chekhov*

This chapter explains why Deep Point-of-View is one of the best editing techniques that you can use to create a realistic setting through sensory details without giving readers a weak or nondescript visual. The tools and tips in this section will demonstrate how writers can revise filter words used in shallower descriptions by transforming the setting into a much stronger visual for their readers.

Locations should become a big part of any story, and not merely be considered by the writer as a place where the story unfolds. As you revise, remember that all characters need to be associated to their settings. Whatever place you create for your character, he/she must live within it. It's not enough to describe the location or scenery at the beginning of the novel, and then let the character wander throughout the scenes without any further connection to his/her environment.

When a writer accurately describes the iridescent glint of a raven's wing or the flaming burst of color from a sunrise, the writer emerges the reader deeply into the story.

The setting is just as important for the reader to imagine as the characters.

All characters need a place to live and breathe and work and roam. The fictional world (or an actual real place) writers create for their characters should not just include a home, workplace, or neighborhood, but a background as well.

When writers are told to add the *setting*, it means much more than just the physical space where the story occurs and the characters dwell. Give readers vital information regarding the setting that include a few additional details, such as the time-period and where the story or scene takes place. A city in the 1950s? A farm in the 1800s? A high-rise in the 1980s? In a galaxy far, far away? In a hellish underground dimension? In a Victorian era?

By incorporating sensory details into a setting, along with vivid descriptions, writers can easily stay in Deeper POV. So, don't tell me that the house was on fire, instead *show* me the blaze and let me feel the heat on my skin.

Four simple techniques to make a setting more visual:

1) Make the landscape active by having characters interact within it.

2) Use color to add an extra depth to the scenery.

3) Make the setting a vital part of the scene.

4) Use the five senses to make the backdrop more realistic.

Sometimes writers need to simply and quickly convey details or information to the reader and move on, but if a writer applies Deeper POV on occasion, then they can bring the reader into the scene as intimately as possible.

For instance, when depicting a location/setting, describe things the way only your unique character sees them through their unique "voice" and include a few significant sensory details.

When writers use "There was" or "There are" at the beginning of a sentence to describe an object or a setting, it creates a weak visual. These words add nothing to the scene, and sentences with these phrases can become wordy and flavorless.

Look at some examples…

SHALLOW: There was a horse and a stack of hay inside the barn.

SHOWING: Within the cozy barn, a black horse chewed quietly on a stack of fragrant hay.

SHALLOW: There are three pictures hung on the wall in a row.

SHOWING: Three framed photos placed in a row on the wall.

SHALLOW: There were five dogs sleeping on the rug.

SHOWING: Five pugs snoozed on the shaggy rug.

***

What usually draws a reader deeply into a story is the use of language and the way a writer describes a setting through the head and heart of their characters. One way to do that is to include a few of the five senses in every scene.

Please study this first example, where the sentence is *telling*...

SHALLOW:

There was a big table in the dining room and it looked like the wood was rotting. When I touched the surface it felt rough and dusty.

Now, the next illustration states the facts while giving readers enough of a visual to "see" the table in their mind's eye and experience the "touch" through sensory details without describing it in a boring way.

(The words considered filtering references are underlined in the first example.)

Here is the revision, where same information is *shown*...

SHOWING:

A wooden table, its surface peeling away like brown bark, sat in the unused dining room. As my fingers trailed along its uneven surface, specks of dust coated my fingertips.

***

Showing is always much more powerful and explicit than just *telling* the reader, but it can often be more wordy. Yet I wouldn't let that hinder your use of this amazing tool. Sure, simply *telling* the reader can be a faster way to convey a lot of details about the setting; however, without sensory details it is usually written in a way that is nondescript and slows the pace.

My advice is to never push "pause" on your story to dump out tedious details or facts regarding the setting or location. Although, I realize with some genres like high-fantasy or science fiction require lots of world-building, the descriptions can still be cleverly woven within the narrative.

DRAMATIC SCENES

Quote: "Let your description unfold as a character moves throughout the scene. Consider which details your character would notice immediately, and which might register more slowly. Let your character encounter those details interactively." — *columnist, Moira Allen, editor of Writing World*

Deep POV just means painting a more vivid picture for your readers through your POV character. How they "see" the world and describe it for the readers is what gives a writer their own unique style and the character its "voice."

When writing in Deeper POV, a writer should always include the five senses and other sensory details to make the scene very visual and more *real* for the reader.

Incorporating Deeper POV in your fiction writing is a great way of making any scene come to life. So remember that applying any of the five senses to a scene will deepen the experience for the reader, and in some cases, even induce an emotional response.

Also, try to include the emotional reactions, internal-dialogue, and physical actions of your characters to spice up your descriptions and avoid a boring list of details.

Here are a few more examples of Deeper POV and how it applies to setting. The shallower sentences are considered *telling* the reader information by writing descriptions in a straightforward manner, which is fine on occasion if needed, but I want to inspire writers to *dig deeper* to make their fictional world as three-dimensional as possible. (The words considered filtering references are underlined.)

Here are some examples I created to illustrate how to vividly describe a setting…

SHALLOW: I thought the forest looked tall and huge.

SHOWING: Within the vast forest, the towering trees swayed in the breeze, their spindly branches waving hello.

SHALLOW: He noticed that the room was sparse and it felt cold.

SHOWING: A chill shivered over his skin. The vacant room seemed lonely and unused.

SHALLOW: There were very tall buildings in this part of the city.

SHOWING: The soaring buildings with their concrete heads in the clouds cast long shadows on the sidewalks below.

SHALLOW: The hillsides looked enormous and they had dry grass.

SHOWING: The rolling hills resembled an endless expanse of balding grey heads.

SHALLOW: There was a bad storm coming.

SHOWING: The horizon lit up with white light followed by the loud grumble of thunder.

SHALLOW: The night <u>looked</u> dark and it had a big moon.

SHOWING: The darkness fell quickly like a shadowy blanket over the land and moonlight struck the sleeping homes like cold silver.

SHALLOW: <u>There were</u> a lot of big, fancy homes in this area.

SHOWING: The area was dominated by impressive mansions with fluted Corinthian columns on the lower and upper stories.

***

Please examine this description of a wooded area...

The forest, disturbingly magnificent and inviting in daylight, seemed disturbingly horrid and repelling at nightfall. Temperatures in October plummeted quickly when the stars became sparkling specks in a naked dismal sky. I thrashed through the undergrowth to avoid walking in the road. But sharp branches whipped at my face and hands, snagging my leather jacket. Birds screeched their frenzied haranguing overhead like cries of the damned. Footsteps pounded behind me.

Oh, god—he'd found me!

I scrambled over fallen tree trunks, and past the tangled area of broken twigs, but I wasn't quick enough. The knife plunged into my shoulder and I fell to the hard ground in a pool of blood.

***

So instead of just describing something in uninteresting detail, writers should try to make the description of a setting as powerful and visual as possible for their readers. As you revise your own work, these examples and advice should help you develop your own style in crafting dynamic settings and locations.

ATMOSPHERE

Quote: "Place matters to me. Invented places matter more."
—*bestselling author, Alice Hoffman*

This chapter will focus on how to add a dash of descriptive atmosphere (mood) to your scenes. One way to do that is by adding an emotional atmosphere and vivid mood into your settings. I challenge writers to describe the setting or location through the characters emotions instead of doing a description info-dump.

One way to do that is for writers to show readers where their characters live, work, and play. To write awesome description, add the five senses to your narrative and use Deep POV to effectively describe a scene.

I urge writers not to describe the setting with a cliché such as, "It was a dark and stormy night..." because settings can establish a distinct mood and atmosphere, like in a gothic novel with a mysterious castle, or a spaceship in a galaxy far, far away. Consider the setting not just as a factual location, but as a crucial part of a story's ambiance and emotional impact.

I'm going to include some examples to show you what I mean by adding mood and atmosphere to your scene descriptions.

Please examine this example…

The room pulsated with dark energy, as if it were alive, breathing and writhing in pain. Or maybe it was mirroring my own tumbling emotions. Beneath my feet, the hardwood floor grumbled with power like a sleeping beast. The loud furnace was its beating heart.

There is something here. I can sense it.

The supernatural power traveled through the stone floor, seeping past my sneakers and into my skin. That's when I knew that the slumbering evil living within the castle had awakened.

***

The above scene was very detailed and set the mood for the storyline.

Here's another short excerpt taken from my novel, *Immortal Eclipse* that illuminates ways a writer can include atmosphere (mood) in their scenes…

Slipping off my boots and socks, I roll up my pants, and walk to the edge of the shore and stand mesmerized by the turbulent ocean. My metallic blue toenails gleam in the sunshine. Dorian is watching me closely, his eyes dark—ravenous. He's biting his lip and his eyes stay on mine. Burning into me. His stare is like a delicious game of sexual torture. My skin warms and blood buzzes in my veins, thrumming loudly in my ears. Heart thumping, I break the intense eye contact, turning away from him to look out at the sea.

In the distance, a sailboat bobbles on the water and seagulls cry like lost children into the surf.

As if angry, the waves crash into the beach, causing me to jump back. Dorian's hungry gaze follows my every move. A few seconds later, another icy wave rolls in and covers my bare feet, my toes sinking into the cold sand. The ocean seems to reflect all the stormy passions raging within me.

***

Notice how closely the character associated her thoughts and feelings with the setting? Did you notice how the atmosphere effected mood and *showed* instead of telling what the characters were thinking and feeling? Could you see where I inserted Deep POV into the narrative to enhance the scene?

Here is another excerpt taken from my book, *Beautifully Broken* that illustrates how to blend the setting with the five senses, along with creating a "mood" in this short scene...

Ariana sped down one street after another, slowing only when the mansion, surrounded by a tall spiked-iron fence, loomed ahead. She parked, and a glance at the glowing dashboard clock said I was fifteen minutes early. The headlights of the Volkswagen illuminated the entrance. Craven Manor was colossal, ancient, and ominous. Shutters were closed, half of them hanging from the windows. The heavy scent of jasmine filled the evening air. Winds stirred the bone-like branches against the sides of the mansion, creating scary scraping noises. An owl hooted. All the spooky place needed was a sign that said: *Hotel Transylvania.*

***

I have included another scene to illustrate using the five senses and written in a Deeper POV taken from one of my novels, *Reckless Revenge...*

Fifteen minutes later, I parked near the arched entrance of Silent Hollows Cemetery. From the glove compartment, I grabbed a flashlight and a squirt gun loaded with holy water. I left the backpack on the seat and decided to scout out a location for the spell, then come back later to retrieve it. Moving toward the cemetery gates, unease zipped along my spine.

Do not panic. It's only a graveyard.

Yeah, right. A *super* dark and spooky graveyard.

The gate gave a rusty moan when I forced it open. From the streetlights around the edge of the fence, deep pockets of shadows fell across the pathway.

Every noise made me flinch and look over my shoulder. I fought overwhelming anxiety. Even with the flashlight on, every shadow moved. At least I didn't have to stress about any lycans showing up—that had to be a good thing.

My gaze darted across the terrain. Cold winds made my teeth grind and my body shiver. The darkness wrapped itself around me quickly and surreptitiously.

Squelching my phobia, I shoved the squirt gun into my pocket and swung the beam of light throughout the shadowy cemetery that was dripping with unseen dangers. The fog heaved like some miasma from hell. Headstones gleamed silver like bony specters. Trees rustled, leaves fell. Something advanced in the rolling fog.

***

Did that give you any ideas on how to revise a scene in your own novel?

This next excerpt is from my novel, *Lost in Starlight* that describes a high school cafeteria, which should help spark your creative muse and show you how to lace "voice" with action and humor and some of the five senses into your scenes.

Please examine this example…

Sunlight trickles through the windows, dancing over the tables and the tacky orange chairs of Haven High's cafeteria. The nauseating odor of greasy pizza wafts from the kitchen area, and the hiss of a soda can opening resonate throughout the crowded space.

My gaze scans over the other students. The designer clothed yuppies cluster in one corner, as if they would rather not socialize with the peasants. Overachievers study instead of eating. Kids-most-likely-to-drop-out take their food and trudge outside. Social rejects are scattered throughout the room. And my group—a mix of geeks, emos, and Goths—are mostly assembled in the back of the room. Some would say that I'm queen of the geekdom, and I wear my invisible crown with honor.

***

Now do you get an idea of how much fun writing description by using atmosphere, the five senses, and Deep POV can be?

Here's one more short example…

The sun crept slowly over the hillside, igniting the dull morning sky with vibrant hues. The golden orb cast warm beams in every direction over the estate. I stared out the window, the rising sun making the colors more vivid with each passing minute. But as beautiful as the morning was, today would be horrible. Someone was going to die…

***

This informative chapter on including a sense of "mood" to your senses that ties in with your character's emotions should inspire you to revise some of your own scenes.

ROOM DESCRIPTION

Quote: "…[if the writer] gives us such details about the streets, stores, weather, politics, and details about the looks, gestures, and experiences of his characters, we cannot help believing that the story is true." —*author of "The Art of Fiction," John Gardner*

To successfully create a great scene, writers should remember to describe the setting at the beginning of each new scene or chapter to help the reader get a visual of the location.

If you effectively describe a room, then you will set the scene and give your readers a clear image of where your characters live and breathe. But don't catalog items or furniture in a room like a boring grocery list. To effectively create a great scene, you need to balance the action of your character with the description of the location. So please get imaginative while describing the interior of the house and all the rooms of the character's home.

For instance, what would he/she see in their bedroom or living room? Tables? Leather sofa? Bunkbed? A desk? A pile of old records? A cushioned recliner?

What objects are inside their home? TV? Dishwasher? Family photos? A stack of books? A computer? Knick-knacks?

What is the character's furnishings like? Modern? Antiques? Comfortable and worn? Wood, pine, oak?

What does the character hear in their home? The percolating of coffee brewing? Music playing? The drip of a leaky faucet? Static from a TV? Video games being played?

What does he/she smell inside their home? Dirty laundry? Fresh baked bread? Minty toothpaste? Burnt toast? Buttery popcorn? Moldy attic? Smelly sweat socks? A citrus air freshener? Leather furniture?

Here are some examples I crafted to illustrate how to vividly describe a street or neighborhood...

SHALLOW: There was a filing cabinet, desk, chair, and lamp.

SHOWING: The office décor appeared old-dated with a rusty filing cabinet leaning to one side, a desk held up by brick legs, a wobbly chair, and a brass lamp covered by a moth eaten shade.

SHALLOW: The kitchen looked large and it felt warm. He smelled chicken baking.

SHOWING: The oven warmed the spacious kitchen, and the spicy aroma of chicken baking filled the space.

SHALLOW: The rooms hadn't been cleaned and there was a bad smell.

SHOWING: The rooms were crammed with thick dust and an awful stink came from a litter box long overdue for a change.

***

Please study this longer example, where the scene is *telling*…

SHALLOW:

The room looked just like she remembered. Holly was instantly transported back to her adolescence because her old bedroom still contained everything from her childhood.

Here is the revision, where same information is *shown*…

SHOWING:

She pushed open the solid oak door and stepped into her childhood bedroom. Light blue striped wallpaper with posters of rock bands covered the walls. A plush azure rug and two overstuffed armchairs flanked a dank fireplace. A queen-sized bed, draped with a sheer curtain dominated the room. The scent of lilacs drifted in the air. Out the single window, the melancholy song of a Blue Jay filled her ears.

Holly leaned a hip against the bulky dresser. Her hand lightly trailed the dust coating its smooth surface and she wiped her fingers off on her jeans. Tears spilled from her big brown eyes. Her heart ached with guilt. This was the last place she'd seen her father, before she'd stormed out the front door twenty years ago.

***

Please study these examples…

SHALLOW: The room was crowded with stuff and it smelled.

SHOWING: The smell of dust and fresh paint assaulted my nostrils with the first step I took through the doorway. Everything within the warehouse appeared faded or washed out despite being lit by fluorescent bulbs secured to the ceiling. The concrete walls were painted a dingy charcoal color like a prison.

***

Here's an example of a room description taken from my novel, *Lost in Starlight* that weaves in emotion, character background, and the five senses into the narrative…

Slinging the strap of my backpack over one shoulder, I climb the stairs to the second-floor, then up another narrow staircase to the third-floor attic. Only one big room up here and it's all mine.

My bedroom has a sloped ceiling with wooden beams arching overhead. Three gothic prints by the talented illustrator Victoria Frances parade over the walls and a poster of my favorite band—*Thirty Seconds to Mars*—hangs over the bed. Sunlight streams through the velvet drapes covering the windows, except for the circular one facing the front of the house.

I stretch my arms over my head and arch my back, dropping my stuff near the closet. A tangy cheese odor emanates from an open bag of Cheetos left on the desk and mingles with the sweet, almost musky, scent of strawberry incense.

For a second, I imagine what Hayden's room looks like. Does he have a drum set? Play that *Rock Band* game with his friends?

Jinx, my black cat, is sprawled across the black and scarlet duvet covering the bed. He lifts his head and meows a greeting. I shuffle past the sticker-encrusted desk that rests under one of the windows and holds my MacBook computer and a small TV with a built-in DVD player—perfect for watching late night horror flicks, and on the shelf above is my beloved collection of Monster High dolls. I drop my cell on the desk and catch sight of the dried funeral wreath drooping over the doorway.

***

Here's a description of a high school gym taken from *Darkness of Light* by Stacey Marie Brown. Please examine this example...

I scanned the decorated gym. Cheesy cardboard cutouts and paper streamers dangled from the ceiling. Red and black balloons and huge paper-mache masks tried to cover up the basketball hoops and the school mascot painted on the walls. It didn't make the gym look any better, nor did it take away the slight stench of sweat and dirty socks.

***

Here's an excerpt taken from *Darkfever* by Karen Marie Moning that is a description of an unusual bookstore. Please examine this example...

I stepped inside and stopped, blinking in astonishment. From the exterior I'd expected a charming little book and curio shop with the inner dimensions of a university Starbucks. What I got was a cavernous interior that housed a display of books that made the library *Disney's* Beast gave to Beauty on their wedding day look understocked.

Still, I'd never imagined a bookstore like this. The room was probably a hundred feet long and forty feet wide. The front half of the store opened all the way up to the roof, four stories or more. Though I couldn't make out the details, a busy mural was painted on the domed ceiling. Bookcases lined each level, from floor to molding. Behind elegant banisters, platform walkways permitted catwalk access on the second, third, and fourth levels. Ladders slid on oiled rollers from one section to the next. The first floor had freestanding shelves arranged in wide aisles to my left, two seating cozies, and a cashier station to my right.

***

Here is one more example I created to illustrate how to vividly describe a room...

I glanced through the doorway into my bedroom. The white walls appeared mostly bare, except for the two brightly colored posters of my favorite rock bands tapped over the canopy bed.

Sunlight filtered through the lace curtains framing the lone window and struck the dusty pine dresser smashed into one corner. A pile of unwashed clothing hulked near the walk-in closet door.

**

Find creative ways to describe your scenes and avoid using filtering words that remove the reader from the experience.

My challenge to you is to rewrite a scene in your novel in Deep POV and try to use at least two of the five senses.

NEIGHBORHOOD DESCRIPTION

Quote: "...setting is more than a mere backdrop for action; it is an interactive aspect of your fictional world that saturates the story with mood, meaning, and thematic connotations."
—*veteran writing instructor, Jessica Morrell*

This chapter focuses on how to effectively describe a suburban town, city street, wooded area, or residential neighborhood. The use of the five senses will allow a reader to enter the scene by inducing an emotional response. It works because it creates imagery and tension within the mind.

Adding descriptive details really doesn't take a lot of extra work, and it's worth it to give your reader a "real" world that they can see, feel, hear, and touch.

One great way of making a scene multi-dimensional is to *dig deeper.* Get creative and describe the neighborhood and people living near the character's home.

For instance, what would he/she see on their street? Buses? Cars? Teens on bicycles? Flowerbeds? Tall trees? A stream? A subway? Trolley cars? Horses and wagons?

Is the street quiet? Noisy? Hectic? A bustling farmer's market? A neglected estate?

What buildings or places are near their home? Apartments? Other houses? Retail stores? A school? A fire department? A playground? Botanical gardens? Soccer field?

What are the character's neighbors like? Friendly? Aloof? Nosy? Loud?

What does the character hear in their neighborhood? Dogs barking? Music from a radio? Cars pulling into a driveway? Kids playing? Garage doors opening or closing? Insects buzzing? Rusty chains on a tree swing? Wind chimes?

What does he/she smell in their hood? Freshly mowed grass? Stinky sewer drains? The sweet scent of honeysuckle? Burning rubber from tires? Wet dog? Smoke from a chimney? Meat cooking on a BBQ? Chlorine from a swimming pool?

Here are some examples I crafted to illustrate how to vividly describe a street or neighborhood...

SHALLOW: The neighborhood and homes looked older.

SHOWING: The sunlight cast a shadow on the gaunt spectral homes in this ancient neighborhood.

SHALLOW: The streets were busy with traffic.

SHOWING: The traffic lurched along the smog burdened streets.

SHALLOW: The houses were quaint and homey looking.

SHOWING: The yellow bungalows facing the tree-lined sidewalk had lush green lawns and softly jingling wind chimes.

***

Here is another example I drafted to demonstrate how to vividly describe a neighborhood…

As I walk out of the quiet, air-conditioned comfort of the bookstore, I'm immediately hit by a blast of hot air from the street. I unzip my windbreaker and tie the sleeves around my waist.

Tall buildings with their concrete heads in the clouds crowd the business district, and the grumble of trucks and cars passing by resemble a congested river of vehicles rushing toward an unknown destination.

I maneuver around a hot dog vendor, wiping his sweaty brow, but bump into office-workers on their lunch break. Smartly dressed men and women hurrying in the direction of a cafe further down the street. The mixture of onion, garlic, pepper, and other spices create a potent combination that tingles my nose.

Holding my breath for a moment, I hurry past the Italian restaurant and cross the street. I've always wondered how the people working inside can stand the odor of garlic. *Ugh*.

At the next corner, I pause, shifting my weight from foot-to-foot while I wait for the signal to blink "walk" before I cross the busy street.

The light changes to green and I step off the curb—right into the path of a black SUV. My body bounces on the hood, pain ripping through my limbs. Shards of glass from the windshield slash into my skull and torso.

When I woke up hours later in the hospital, my head is bandaged and I'm sporting a white plaster cast on my left leg. The sterile, white room reeks of disinfectant and strong soap.

***

Could you vividly imagine the setting in that scene? Visualize the busy city streets? Smell the aroma of spices?

Please examine this description of a derelict neighborhood…

The walk home through the dimly lit streets wasn't enough to drive out the guilt plaguing him. Charlie ambled to the corner, turned, and began walking at a moderate pace. He didn't pause as he rubbed his arms against the icy winds sweeping the neighborhood. The sun dipped downward in the distance as darkness edged over the land.

Taking stock of his surroundings, Charlie increased his pace. This shortcut had lead him into a dilapidated part of the city. Storefronts with the occasional apartment above yielded to rundown, graffiti covered buildings with busted-out windows and sagging doors. The sidewalk whittled down to barely a few feet wide and became increasingly trash-littered with every step.

He wondered if this part of the city had become derelict because the businesses had moved out or because the gangs had moved in.

Who knew what lurked behind those broken windows. Or what crouched beyond that half-opened door.

He wrinkled his nose at the stench of the sewers. One building had a crumbling smokestack that stretched upward, melting into the overcast sky. He hurried past an abandoned car with the driver's door left ajar.

The street was eerily quiet. Just the hushed muffle of his footsteps and the slow dripping of gutters emptying into drainpipes.

A homeless woman pushing a shopping cart shuffled past him. Her eyes narrowed on his face. "You lost, Mister?"

Charlie ignored her and kept walking, hugging himself against the cold.

***

Did you grasp how that scene was very detailed to set the mood for the storyline?

It is vital to describe where your characters live, work, and play. This chapter should inspire your creative muse and help edit boring scenes into tangible descriptions that the reader can experience and visualize.

BUILDING DESCRIPTIONS

This chapter features ways to describe buildings and homes. As you revise, keep in mind that a clear image of the setting allows readers to "see" it as more realistic. A more specific depiction with vivid, sensory details is the best way to describe a structure or residence.

However, if a writer describes the settings without any of the five senses, a reader doesn't get a vibrant impression of the buildings or the character's home. So I encourage writers to get inventive when describing the buildings surrounding the character's workplace or residence.

For instance, what hat would he/she see out their windows at work or school or home? Bungalows? Metal crates? Warehouses? Buildings shackled with ivy? Stone constructions?

What objects or views would the character notice? Broken windows? Flaking paint? Wraparound porches? Brick facades? Glass walls? Parking lots? Neon signs? Billboards? Chain-link fences?

What style of architecture are the buildings? Space pods? Classic contemporary? Log cabins? Track housing? Concrete structures?

What does the character hear? Birds chirping from a rooftop? The swoosh of a revolving door? People coming and going from a high-rise building?

What does he/she smell? Rust? Fresh paint? Musty odors? Glass cleaner?

Here are some examples I crafted to illustrate how to vividly describe a street or neighborhood…

SHALLOW: The barn looked old.

SHOWING: The red barn wilted in the field strangled with overgrown weeds, its paint peeling and its doors hanging off the rusty hinges.

SHALLOW: The buildings looked tall and made of glass.

SHOWING: The skyscrapers stood like modern stalagmites within the beige smog.

SHALLOW: The houses were contemporary in this part of town.

SHOWING: The suburban homes resembled identical twins in this residential section of town.

SHALLOW: The structure looked like a fort.

SHOWING: The older brick edifice seemed to be guarding a long forgotten past.

***

Which sentence created a more powerful imagine in your mind?

Here are some more examples I drafted to illustrate how to vividly describe a building or house.

Please examine this first description of an abandoned building...

The desolated Victorian ruin sat regally beyond the wrought-iron fence like a house from an antebellum storybook. The ocher peeling paint had been damaged by harsh winters and the broken windows were dusty and festooned with decaying cobwebs. Rambling roof shingles fell from their high perch and a grove of dead trees surrounded the decaying estate.

***

This next example is a scene taken from my short story, CRAVEN MANOR that should give writers some ideas on how to use description to not only paint a vivid picture in the reader's mind, but ways to include "mood" and atmosphere.

Please carefully examine this scene...

Crickets sang and dragonflies buzzed at the entrance. Grass grew wild and tall in the yard, sprouting through cracks in the cement path leading to the portico. The sprawling Gothic mansion blotted out the sun. Tattered shingles from the wilting structure scattered across the lawn.

Outwardly, the manor had a formidable appeal, constructed with a fusion of architectural styles, which closely resembled the features of an American Carpenter Gothic design, often characterized by steep gables and pointed windows. The mansion's walls were long and high and its towers peaked above the staggered trees. The building constructed with cupolas and spires and scrolled balconies—*everything* except gargoyles. Black wrought-iron embellishments, storm shutters, and of course, the obligatory lightning rod atop the tallest tower donned it as a stereotypical-looking haunted house.

***

Please examine this example…

SHALLOW: I saw a farmhouse in the darkness, and then a car came along and almost ran me over.

SHOWING:

I stumbled in the darkness through the brambles.

This is really creepy.

There was an old farmhouse somewhere near Maple Drive. I'd be okay if I could just find the path. Suddenly lights shone in my eyes, blinding me. The crunch of tires on the gravel road caused me to freeze in my tracks.

The headlights came straight toward me. I leaped out of the way just as the rusty Buick drove past.

***

Please carefully examine this next example…

Chase walked warily up to the log cabin and paused beneath a dirty window. Lifting his head and peeking inside, he glimpsed a room filled with dusty old furniture. Everything appeared outdated and worn.

Going around to the porch, he jiggled the brass doorknob. The door slowly creaked opened and the stench of mold and neglect hit his nostrils. He sneezed and the sound echoed throughout the lonely room. Oak floors and banisters gleamed dully in the sunshine.

Please carefully examine this last example taken from my novel, *Immortal Eclipse*…

I hobble along, relieved when a remarkable castle-like building appears, the wood and stone facade speckled with hazy afternoon sunshine.

The mansion stands outlined against the sky, like a hand uplifted in warning, its huge frame dwarfing the pines that form a grove near the property. Weeds and dandelions poke through the cracks in the cobblestone walkway. The impressive mansion resembles a stone bastion from a fairy tale sitting majestically on a cliff above the sea. Its front yard even has the requisite wild and overgrown garden. Dry leaves scuttle and dance across the lawn. A rusty widow's walk, with an enclosed cupola, juts out from one side of the roof.

***

Deeper POV allows a reader to actively participate in the scene and ignites the reader's imagination, as well as helps them to forget that they're *just* reading a story. And a reader who feels like they're vividly experiencing the narrative is a reader who won't be able to put your story down.

CITY DESCRIPTIONS

Whether your story takes place in a real location, or a fictional world, or a distant planet, it's important to include details about the cities, towns, and areas where your characters roam. This chapter illustrates ways a writer can describe cities and locales within the narrative.

For instance, if writers describe the city or area in a nondescript way, a reader doesn't get a vivid image of the location. So I want to inspire writers to get original when depicting the city or town where the character's live.

For instance, what would he/she see out their windows at work or school? Skyscrapers? Victorians? Suburbia? Tree-lined streets? Gravel roads? Spaceships? Corn fields? A vast ocean? Railroad tracks? A quiet village?

What objects would the character notice? Fire hydrants? People walking dogs? A taco truck? A newspaper stand? Plants and trees? Cracked sidewalks? Homeless people? Graffiti? Department stores? Hard concrete landscapes? A derelict alley? A congested freeway?

What do the buildings look like? Modern? A historical district? Urban decay? Gothic revival?

And what buildings would the character view from their workplace or home? A hospital? Church? Grocery store? Shopping center? Barber shop? Florist? Restaurants? Factory? Bus stop? Motels?

What does the character hear in their hometown? Big trucks rumbling by? Horns honking? Police car sirens? Birds singing? Waterfalls gurgling? People talking on cell phones?

What does he/she smell within this fictional world? Rotten garbage? Stinky cigarettes? Burning leaves? Car exhaust? The aroma of restaurants?

Here are some examples I crafted to illustrate how to vividly describe a street or neighborhood...

SHALLOW: I lived near the docks in San Francisco.

SHOWING: I lived along the brawling, noisy, fish-smelling San Francisco docks.

SHALLOW: A picturesque, southern town.

SHOWING: The enchanting, southern town had a rustic appeal.

SHALLOW: Tom stayed in a dumpy motel in a small Mexican town.

SHOWING: Tom stayed overnight in a dusty Mexican town, and slept in a motel that should've been called "El Not-so Grande."

SHALLOW: He walked down the narrow and quiet street.

SHOWING: He ambled down the uneven pavement, the houses lining the street appearing dark and uninhabited.

***

Which sentence created a more powerful imagine in your mind?

As the narrative progresses, writers should introduce only the elements relevant to the scene, the theme, the characters, and the plot. Whenever a writer is describing the setting, they should include action and "voice" and sensory details.

This next excerpt is from my novel, *Beautifully Broken* and illustrates the description of a suburban town…

Living on the dismal northern shores of California, Marin County was always foggy and rarely warm. Glimpses of the sun were erratic in Fallen Oaks. A small town crammed with old Victorian houses, dewy forests, and silver skies. Cell phones, email, and high-speed Internet were definitely around, but life moved slower here. And people gossiped far too much and held grudges forever, often for generations. *Small towns—gotta love them.*

To an outsider, the touristy part of town looked picturesque and historically elegant. People often imagined a quaint coastal town with sandy beaches, sunshine, natural beauty, and affluence.

What outsiders didn't visualize was the darker parts.

The lingering gloom. Deep fog that hovered even during the summer months. Chilly winds from the Bay that seeped into your bones, and froze your fingers and toes. Or the surrounding forest, deep and vast, steeped in shadow and clustered with towering Redwoods; large mammoths of green foliage bunched over, bent and stooped, drenching unexplainable darkness across the land. Gloomy skies, scribbled with clouds that hung oppressively low until the penetration of sunlight was noticeably less.

With its overcast skies, a cursed town like Fallen Oaks was the perfect place for shadow people. Well, most paranormals would love it here, but witches settled here first.

***

After reading that excerpt could you picture the town in your mind? Do you get a real sense of the atmosphere and mood?

Here is another scene to carefully examine…

SHOWING:

As Marc ambled down Redwood Street, the soft meow of a kitten caught his attention. He paused, gazing up and down the street. No sign of any cat. Then he glanced down at the sewer grate just as the yowling intensified.

He crouched and lifted the manhole cover aside and dusted his hands off on his jeans. He leaned over the opening and squinted into the darkness.

A strong whiff of urine and rotten food struck his senses and he recoiled. From his back pocket, Marc removed his keyring that had a small flashlight attached to it and shone light into the hole. Staring up at him was a grimy white kitten. Marc sighed. He couldn't leave the helpless animal down in that dank, dark place.

Marc put the flashlight back into his pocket, and jumped into the gap. His boots hit the murky bottom with a loud splash.

The grumble of passing cars and trucks on the road above him echoed throughout the tunnel. Pulling out his flashlight again, he shined it around the cesspool. A damp moss clung to walls and ceiling. The kitten rubbed against his leg and purred. Reaching down, Marc gently lifted up the poor creature and placed the sodden animal inside his plaid button-up shirt to keep her warm. Spying a rusty ladder, he climbed back out and smiled at successfully rescuing his new feline friend.

***

In the next two chapters, I'll illustrate how to blend color into your settings, which will provide the readers with a vivid imaginary.

COLOR DESCRIPTIONS

This chapter on color should help add spice and vibrancy to all of your descriptions. With a dash of creativity, it is possible to improve anyone's writing by replacing boring word choices with more imaginative ones.

I find as I edit for other writers that the laziest words are produced when describing scenes or characters that include a colors.

Effectively written description can present a clear visual for your reader. By creating a vivid image in the reader's mind, they will actually "see" exactly what you're describing. And using color to paint that picture is what a real artist does!

Add a dash of color to all of your settings and descriptions. Color is everywhere, and it's the easiest way to add some creative sizzle to an otherwise bland description. *Be creative.* I suggest that writers buy a box of crayons and use the names as inspiration. Or go online to visit a paint store and browse all the creative hues and differing shades. Use a Thesaurus to insert unique colors into your scenes. Choose the right word, and your reader will have an instant association.

However, avoid generic words for colors that give vague descriptions as opposed to specific information about the color. Brown eyes don't spark the reader's imagination as deeply as *bronze eyes* or *his gaze was the color of bark*. As writers, we have to describe skin tones, hair, eye color, clothing, and settings, so by including multi-colored descriptors, it can enhance the realism of your fictional world.

Here are a few color examples…

SHALLOW: She wore a red blouse.

SHOWING: Her ruby blouse had a silky sheen.

SHALLOW: His eyes were brown.

SHOWING: His eyes were deep and lustrous, like moonlight sparkling on a forest pond under the shade of ancient oaks.

SHALLOW: The sky was blue.

SHOWING: The sky was a vast sea of cobalt dotted with silvery clouds.

The shallow examples are lifeless and not very imaginative. They don't really tell the reader anything about the scene.

Writers shouldn't use weak descriptions such as *the dog was black* or *her hair was blond*. Introduce depth and texture by saying the *Rottweiler was the shade of midnight* or *her hair was the color of golden sunshine*.

Here's an excerpt taken from my novel, *Lost in Starlight* that demonstrates ways to add color and a Deeper POV to your scenes…

The ornate gate issues a rusty moan as I push it open. When I pass through, a sense of peacefulness instantly whooshes over me. My gaze darts across the emerald terrain. It's a lovely spring day with bursts of yellow daffodils poking their pretty heads out of the ground. The scent of freshly cut grass blends with the aroma of rotting roses. Granite tombstones reflect the golden sunlight and mausoleums—housing the dead—stand proudly.

***

Fiction means bringing settings and character descriptions to life throughout the narrative. One issue many writers struggle with is finding ways to describe colors, or neglecting to add it to the setting at all. This list below can be used to describe eye color, hair, clothing, objects, setting, and even climate.

List of descriptive colors and shades:

Cream: yellowish white, light tint of yellow or buff

Lemon: clear, light yellow

Golden: also gold

Wheaten: fawn or pale yellow

Apricot: pinkish yellow or yellowish pink

Mustard: yellowish brown

Biscuit: pale brown

Fawn: light yellowish brown

Fallow: pale yellow, light brown

Beige: very light brown, light gray with brownish tint

Tan: light brown

Buff: yellowish brown of medium to dark tan

Tawny: dark yellowish or dull yellowish brown

Bronze: a metallic brownish color

Sandy: yellowish red

Copper: metallic reddish-brown

Sorrel: light reddish brown

Bay: reddish brown

Rust Red: reddish yellow; reddish brown

Ruby Red: deep red; carmine

Mahogany: reddish brown

Liver: dark reddish brown

Chocolate: dark brown

Dark Brown

Coffee brown

Dun: dull, grayish brown

Light Gray

Mouse: dark brownish gray

Gray: color of ash

Grizzle: gray, devoid of hue

Iron gray: silver-white metallic gray

Slate gray: a dull dark bluish gray

Blue: dark gray

Sable: dark brown, almost black

Black: ebony

***

This next list can be used to describe hair colors, too. If you write in genres such as fantasy, science fiction, horror, or paranormal romance, then often times a character will have an exotic color to their skin or hair or eyes. Please include this list as a multipurpose reference in your writer's toolbox.

List of evocative and exotic colors:

Framboise

Tanager

Tuberose

Yarrow

Jacaranda

Lobelia

Mesclun

Amaryllis

Cyclamen

Azalea

Jonquil

Lacewing

Frangipane

Alyssum

Verbena

Citrine

Saguaro

Reynard

Nankeen

Arugula

Armagnac

Persimmon

Shagreen

Alabaster

Amethyst

Carnelian

Cinnamon

Coral

Crimson

Ebony

Emerald

Fawn

Indigo

Lavender

Lilac

Scarlett

Sienna

Silver

Auburn

Azure

Cobalt

Granite

Gray

Slate

Teal

Topaz

***

This chapter should be used as a handy wordlist whenever a writer wants to add a splash of color to their scenes.

In the next several chapters, I'll discuss how to merge the weather into your scenes, which will give your readers a strong depiction of the setting within your amazing fictional world.

WEATHER DESCRIPTION

This chapter features ways to insert the description of the weather into your narrative. Weather can be a significant element when describing a setting. And certain weather conditions can undoubtedly affect people's mood, such as a drab, rainy day might make a character feel depressed, or a bright, sunny day might lift their spirits.

Weather can also become a clever plot devise if used for external conflict, such as *Man versus Nature,* or even if it forecasts (pun not intended) some foreshadowing.

When writers describe an outdoor scene or a character goes outside, ask yourself this: Is it raining, cloudy, wintry, or sunshiny? Hot or cold? Damp or humid? Are the skies a clear blue or a drab grey? Is the air smoggy or fresh with the scent of rain?

Weather can be a powerful way to enhance any scene, and incorporate atmosphere and mood. The right blend of description, introspection, climate, and action can create a strong image for the reader. A great weather description adds tension, emotion, and underlying ambiance. But poorly written descriptions can leave the reader grappling for a visual and feeling disconnected from the characters and the story.

Additionally, don't forget to add the sense of *smell* to any of your outdoor scenes, and use it to make the climate or the season more realistic.

Also, writers can use the weather to bring forth strong emotions or reactions in your characters, where the weather plays a significant role. For instance, in a Gothic tale, it would have a billowy fog, flashes of lightning, and shrieking winds. Cold, damp earthy smells and the scent of wet stone in the castle.

Descriptions of weather are most effective when it's discernible, aromatic, and tangible. For instance, writers could describe a hailstorm or a snowfall, an extreme heat wave, or dense twisting fog, or a rainbow after a heavy rain in any type of genre.

Here are some examples I drafted to illustrate how to vividly describe the weather…

SHALLOW: It was a cold, ugly day.

SHOWING: The harsh winds shook the trees as the foreboding clouds rolled in.

SHALLOW: It was a sunny day.

SHOWING: The sun shone brightly from a clear cerulean sky.

SHALLOW: A storm was brewing.

SHOWING: A thunderclap pealed and icy raindrops splattered the pavement.

***

Fiction writers can use natural elements to illustrate the climate by creating a conflicting effect within an outdoor setting. For instance, a funeral can take place on a bright sunny day, or a wedding during a freak thunderstorm.

To illustrate my point, I have included this excerpt from my novel, *Moonlight Mayhem*. Please examine this example of a weather description...

On a brisk September morning, we buried my dad.

Nestled amid hundred-year-old pines, grassy knolls, and manicured walkways, the Silent Hollows Cemetery appeared serene. Birds chirped happily in the trees. Flowers lazed in the warm sunlight. Not an ominous cloud in sight, or heavy mist covering the ground. The languid days of summer had vanished. As had picnics, fireflies, and watching baseball games in the park with my dad. Most of my childhood memories were packed with his love and humor, and the certainty that if my dad were around even the darkest of storms would eventually pass.

A dazzling jet blue sky brimming with dazzling sunshine wasn't the type of day you buried someone you loved.

Darrah and I trudged past headstones and mausoleums. The graveyard reeked of damp earth and rotting roses. The other mourners, including Ariana and Pastor Williams, had already gathered around the mahogany coffin shrouded by a mound of flowers. Everyone had dressed in mourning attire, but only

Darrah managed to look chic, wearing a black silk dress that hugged her body and plunged low enough to show the top of her boobs. Totally inappropriate for a funeral.

Darrah squinted and slipped on a pair of designer sunglasses. She despised the sun. Thought it was too bright, too happy. At present, I agreed.

***

Being an avid reader, I depend on the scene's description to take me away to faraway lands and exciting locations. I love being able to step into someone else's life for a while and see it through their eyes. Like I said, one way to set the scene is to include the weather.

Now, my challenge to you is to find at least three scenes in your manuscript and add a brief description of the weather to each of them.

Below is an excerpt from my novel, *Beautifully Broken* to give you an idea on how to effectively add weather and the season into any scene.

Please study this example of a weather description…

Thick ground fog swaddled the neighborhood. An early morning hush settled over the town, the drizzling mist softening the streets. I drank in the brisk morning air, welcoming the chill of winter on my flushed cheeks.

This next excerpt was taken from my novel, *Moonlight Mayhem*, which illustrates on how to enhance your scene with mood and a weather…

A golden sun was swept away by ominous gray clouds. The neighborhood appeared barren; the trees looked like dismembered hands clawing at the ashen sky and the cracked sidewalks deserted. The screeching wind rustled through the autumn trees and dry leaves were tossed and blown like tumbleweeds across the front yard.

Please study this last example of weather…

Nancy stared out the window at the dreary world outside. Faint pitter-patter clatters hit the roof. The wind was whistling as lightning struck the gloomy sky. Winds jerked at the trees, and raindrops left zigzag trails down the foggy glass. A large boom reverberated in distant hillside, and she couldn't help but flinch at the loud rumble of the clap. Pulling a blanket over her shoulders, she hoped that Devon made it home okay in the thunderstorm.

Please read this next example of a weather description…

The looming silence was broken when a hiss of wind spun before the gates, and a shadowed figure of a man stepped forward. Staring out the window, Kate jerked back in fright.

Without breaking pace, the tall man took long strides toward the front door of the manor, the moon glimmering faintly off his dark hair, thrashing in the wind.

***

This chapter should help writers to revise their own scenes and inspire them to include details regarding the weather in their settings.

COLD WEATHER

Now, some of you might think "Why bother describing the weather?" Well, one reason is because it can add an extra layer of realism to the setting and even create a *mood* (atmospheric), or even tie in with your theme.

Don't dismiss its importance to your descriptions. Weather can provide an effective element in any type of setting.

If a writer tells the reader that it was a cold day, it is considered shallower writing. Writers should find innovative ways to *show* through Deeper POV instead.

Everything a writer needs to set the scene and vividly describe a location for the reader can be accomplished by using sensory details. As a writer revises a scene, it is effective to imagine themselves in the actual location, and then think about the details. *What is the character seeing, smelling, hearing, and touching?* Using the five senses is mandatory when a writer wants to put a clear, descriptive visual into the reader's mind.

Examples of cold weather for settings:

Frost on the windows

Howling winds

Birds flying south

Heavy fog

Overcast skies

Spiders spinning larger than usual webs

Ice on the ground

Icicles hanging from roof

Slick roads

Harsh rains

Bare trees

Somber clouds

***

Here are some examples I drafted to illustrate how to describe cold weather...

SHALLOW: The weather was cold and cloudy.

SHOWING: The trembling sky was full of tumultuous clouds.

SHALLOW: It was a dismal afternoon and it looked like it was going to rain.

SHOWING: The bleak afternoon embraced grey skies, threatening rain.

SHALLOW: Outside it was raining.

SHOWING: Ominous, black clouds released a downpour.

***

I have included a wordlist to use as a reference whenever a writer is describing a colder climate.

Cold Weather Adjectives:

Below Zero

Arctic

Bare

Barren

Biting

Bitter Cold

Bleak

Blustery

Chilling

Chilly

Cloudy

Cold

Cozy

Crackling

Crisp

Crunchy

Crystalline

Dark

Dead

Depressing

Desolate

Dismal

Drafty

Dreary

Drenched

Enchanted

Extreme

Fluffy

Foggy

Freezing

Frigid

Frostbitten

Frosty

Frozen

Glacial

Glistening

Gray

Gusty

Harsh

Hazy

Howling

Hypothermic

Ice Cold

Icy

Insulated

Intensifying

Isolated

Knee-Deep

Leafless

Lonely

Melting

Misty

Nippy

Northern

Numb

Overcast

Polar

Powdery

Rainy

Relentless

Sedentary

Severe

Shivering

Slippery

Slushy

Snowbound

Sparkling

Thaw

Windy

Wintertime

Wintery

Wintry

Woolen

Zippy

***

Here are two descriptions of cold weather taken from my novel, *Moonlight Mayhem*...

The night air was cold and crisp and the weeping willow tree swayed in the breeze, leaves falling from the branches like autumn rain. Every shadow seemed to shift and stretch.

Here is the other description of weather...

Solemn clouds, elongating and unyielding, weaved across the sun, and drained the happiness from my day. Only gloomy skies, weak sunshine, and creeping fog. Another typical day in Ravenwood.

***

I have included an excerpt taken from my new adult novel, *Smash Into You* that depicts the weather...

When I walked out of Stevenson Hall and into the bright morning sunlight loaded with books the next day, the chilly winds slapped my cheeks.

***

Vivid, sensory descriptions are the most essential element in a setting. It allows the reader to visualize the setting through your descriptive details and through the senses.

Along with providing details to the setting, weather is one of the easiest ways to cement the reader in the scene and hint at the mood.

WARM WEATHER

Sometimes including the weather in the setting can be a benevolent, even a genial element, and other times Mother Nature can rage and behave like an antagonist, forcing the characters to fight for survival.

Certain types of genres require varied levels of detail when establishing the setting and world-building. For example, a high-fantasy, historical adventure, or a science fiction novel will have an observant readership that expects not only graphic details and powerful imaginary regarding the setting, but facts and accuracy, too.

One way to convey the weather or depict the setting is to have a character describe the background in his/her own "voice" through the five senses, rather than using an omniscient POV.

Examples of warm weather for settings:

Wilting flowers

Brown, dead grass

Cloudless sky

Bright, hot sun

Humid

Dry winds

Sizzling asphalt

Air-conditioned house

Condensation on glasses

Sunburned faces / bodies

Muggy heat

***

Here are some examples I drafted to illustrate how to describe warm weather...

SHALLOW: It was a hot, sunny day.

SHOWING: The balmy breeze stroked our skin like a fiery furnace.

SHALLOW: The weather turned warmer.

SHOWING: The sun blazed, drowning the world in a flood of golden warmth.

SHALLOW: The day was warm and bright.

SHOWING: Bright and vivid sunlight warmed the earth.

***

I have included a glossary to use as a reference whenever a writer is describing a warmer environment.

Warm Weather Adjectives:

Ablaze

Air-Conditioned

Balmy

Blazing

Blistering

Boiling

Breezy

Bright

Burning

Clammy

Clear

Cloudless

Endless

Fragrant

Green

Happy

Hazy

Hot

Humid

Oppressive

Red Hot

Ripe

Roasting

Scorching

Sizzling

Steamy

Sticky

Stifling

Sultry

Summery

Sun-Drenched

Sun-Filled

Sun-Kissed

Sunburnt

Sunny

Sweaty

Sweltering

Toasty

Tan

Tropical

Unforgettable

Verdant

Warm

***

I have included an example that depicts the warmer weather...

SHOWING:

The sun flared down like a raging fire from a cloudless cobalt sky. Zoey's skin heated up like a pie baking in an oven every time she stepped outside. If only they had a pool...

She stood behind the sliding glass-doors and sighed. The roses in the backyard wilted and sagged on the vines. The lawn appeared shriveled and russet. Her neighbors hide inside their own dark houses to find a cool solace from the blistering summer heat.

***

I want to encourage writers reading this guide to include a sentence or two about the weather in any outdoor scenes.

NIGHTTIME

As a fiction writer, you are the artist and landscaper doing the world-building within your reader's imagination. Be inspired to welcome the magnificence of description by applying dramatic attention to every detail in your individual settings.

Writers should include a few vital details about the location by lacing the description throughout the dialogue and action to remind the reader where the scene takes place. And including the time of day in your scenes will also help to convey the passing of time.

List of general times:

Evening

Nightfall

Sundown

Late afternoon

Midnight

Dusk

Twilight

Dinner

Sunset

Full Moon

***

And whenever a writer describes something, try to see if it can be revised more effectively through character actions, like in the examples below. These sentences should help writers get a clear idea on how to write a descriptive scene.

Here are some examples I drafted to illustrate how to vividly describe evening…

SHALLOW: The sunset looked gold.

SHOWING: As the sun set, the lingering clouds turned a shimmering gold.

SHALLOW: There was a big moon over the neighborhood.

SHOWING: The full moon bathed the neighborhood with a luminous glow.

SHALLOW: The sky darkened and filled with clouds.

SHOWING: Wispy clouds drifted lazily across the night sky.

SHALLOW: The night was cold and dark.

SHOWING: A cool breeze fingered through the trees as night's veil fell upon the sleeping world.

SHALLOW: There was a moon shaped crescent over the lake.

SHOWING: The crescent moon glistened over the sparkling lake.

***

Words to describe night or darkness or black:

Caliginosity

Darkness

Dead of Night

Dimness

Evening

Gloom

Murkiness

Nightfall

Nighttime

Obscurity

Opacity

Semidarkness

Shade

Shadows

Twilight

Cimmerian

Aphotic

Black /Blackish

Caliginous

Clouded / Cloudy

Crepuscular

Dingy

Dusk / Dusky

Faint

Foggy

Indistinct

Inky

Misty

Murky

Nebulous

Eclipse

Obscure

Opaque

Overcast

Pitch-Black

Darkness

Pitchy

Rayless

Shaded

Shadowy

Somber

Sooty

Stygian

Sunless

Tenebrous

Obscure

Vague

Gloaming

Lugubrious

Nyctophobia

Nocturnal

Stygian

Tenebrous

***

This excerpt was taken from my novel, *Moonlight Mayhem* describes a nighttime setting...

Outside, the buildings gleamed bleakly beneath filtered light from the streetlamps and a full moon occupied the painfully dark sky. Splotches of blood stained the sidewalk. Still wet and running between the cracks in the pavement, like a river of crimson.

The excerpt was taken from my novel, *Reckless Revenge*...

Beyond the back fence, giant redwoods soared to heights that seemed to touch the clouds. Cold, inky darkness inched closer to the house, and a tremor slid through my limbs.

At night, most things went to bed. But *scary* things woke up for playtime. Especially living in Ravenwood, where they could hide in the habitual fog that drifted over from the San Francisco Bay.

My boyfriend, Trent Donovan—all tall and buffed and smoking hot—and I had been busy making out when branches at the edge of the yard parted and chilling howls pierced the night air. Not coyotes or wolves. This was Northern California. And it wasn't something natural, either. More like a paranormal with a perverse bloodlust.

The excerpt was taken from my novel, *Shattered Silence*...

I gazed out the windshield. Shadows tumbled on the road as the sun waned. Not safe in Ravenwood after sundown. Streetlights blinked on like sour fluorescent streaks oozing onto the roads. Fog hung thickly throughout the darkening terrain. The failing sunlight impaled a yellow glow on the neighborhood. The pines, thick and ancient, seemed to stir with the whisper of magick. Such a thin veneer between this realm and the supernatural one.

***

Could you grasp how the scenes depicted nightfall and darkness?

Words and phrases with powerful sensory connotations always increase the chances of producing an empathic response in the reader.

DAYTIME

Whether writers are crafting a short story, fanfiction, or an epic historical novel, fictional moments pass just like real time passes. It's important to mention the passing of time in your narrative whenever the story jumps forward in time or a there's a new scene.

And to avoid plot holes in your timeline of events, it might help to include time markers. In other words, I think it's crucial to a story's timeline to include the time of day whenever a new scene takes place or there's a new chapter.

List of general times:

Sunup

Daybreak

Morning

Daylight

Afternoon

Dawn

Breakfast

Brunch

Lunch

Sunrise

Here are some examples I drafted to illustrate how to vividly describe daytime…

SHALLOW: The morning sun rose on the hillside.

SHOWING: The sun rose, staining the hillside in shades of crimson and gold.

SHALLOW: It was afternoon on a cloudy day.

SHOWING: The afternoon clouds crowded the grey skies.

SHALLOW: I watched the sunrise.

SHOWING: An auburn globe rose in the distance.

SHALLOW: That afternoon, it felt cold and dreary.

SHOWING: The afternoon sky was burdened with unbroken dreary clouds.

SHALLOW: The sunshine was bright on the car.

SHOWING: A ray of sunshine glistened off the windshield.

***

Words to describe light or daytime or sunshine:

Sunny

Resplendent

Vivid

Unclouded

Burnished

Ablaze

Actinic

Clear

Cloudless

Abundant

Blinding

Bright

Dappled

Dazzling

Diffused

Filtered

Glaring

Glorious

Golden

Hazy

Indirect

Intense

Mellow

Streaming

Vivid

Gleaming

Glimmering

Glinting

Glittering

Illuminating

Incandescent

Iridescent

Lucent

Luminescent / Luminous

Lustrous

Opalescent

Penumbral

Phosphorescent

Prismatic

Radiant

Resplendent

Scintillating

Shimmering

***

The excerpt was taken from my novel, *Moonlight Mayhem* that describes the setting. Please carefully study this example...

The sun resembled a distant gold coin against the pale, cobalt sky. The graveyard with its endless drab, gray headstones was now empty, void of life, except for Trent and me. And I liked it that way.

***

Here is another example from my novella, FORBIDDEN NIGHT to illustrate how to describe day...

Siobhan skipped breakfast, hopped into her car, a blue Camry, and drove to the local college. Out the car windows, lawns were russet, birch and pine trees stood in abundance, and spring flowers were struggling to reach the sun. Morning fog lingered as if clouds had fallen from the sky and blanketed the earth, making Silent Hills overcast and gloomy. She passed silent, melancholy clusters of weathered houses shackled with ivy, among ancient shade trees.

***

Some things to continuously consider whenever you're revising the setting:

Do the word choices paint vivid images in the reader's mind?

Do the descriptions place the reader in the scene?

Do they make the reader an active participant in the story instead of a mere observer?

It's easy for writers in early drafts to depend on simple, straightforward descriptions of rooms and settings. Using Deep POV does add more words to your scenes, but the experience you'll give your readers will be well worth it.

SEASONS

When describing locations within your marvelous fictional world, it's a good idea to include a mention of the season.

Each season is distinctive and not only affects the weather and nature herself, but it also signals important events during our calendar year. Writers should consider the weather, province, and holidays in the timeline while describing the setting or world-building.

Reveal to readers your fictional world by showing them a man delivering newspapers or garbage cans lined up by the curb. Let the reader see, hear, and touch your scenes. Too many writers let their characters float around in space. Firmly attach them to your world. This is called world-building.

Each new scene needs to establish where the characters are or your readers cannot visualize the setting or where the scene takes place. One way to do that is to include a mention of the seasons.

Here are some examples I drafted to illustrate how to include the season...

SHALLOW: It was the season of Halloween in October.

SHOWING: The trick-or-treaters shrieked and giggled on the porch as they waited for me to open the door with candy.

SHALLOW: It was Thanksgiving and I had to make the meal.

SHOWING: The scents of cinnamon, cloves, and margarine wafted in the kitchen as I prepared the Thanksgiving meal.

SHALLOW: The gym had been decorated for Valentine's Day.

SHOWING: Pink paper hearts fluttered in the air-conditioned breeze in the gymnasium.

SHALLOW: When I walked outside, I smelled pine trees.

SHOWING: The essence of pine floated on the autumn winds.

SHALLOW: It was springtime and flowers were everywhere.

SHOWING: The rural hillside was covered in spring's flourish of poppies.

***

I have included a directory of different holidays that might affect your story's setting or timeline.

List of holidays to consider depending on the season:

A New Year

Valentine's Day

Easter

Mother's Day

Father's Day

Halloween

Thanksgiving

Christmas

New Year's Day

Memorial Day

Independence Day

Labor Day

St. Patrick's Day

Chanukah/Hanukkah

April Fool's Day

Good Friday

Veterans Day

Fourth of July

List of social events to consider:

Wedding

Anniversary

Birthday Party

Birth

Bar Mitzvah

Sweet Sixteen

Funeral

Graduation

Charity Ball / Fundraiser

High School Reunion

Concert

School Dance

Housewarming Party

Bridal Shower

Bachelor Party

***

Please keep in mind while you're rewriting certain scenes in your fictional tale to ensure that the timeline accurately conveys the seasons, any celebrations, and holidays.

SEASONAL SCENTS

Quote: "I love the rewriting and redrafting process. Once I have a first draft, I print the whole thing out and do the first pass with handwritten notes. I write all kinds of notes in the margins and scribble and cross things out. I note down new scenes that need writing, continuity issues, problems with characters and much more. That first pass usually takes a while. Then I go back and start a major rewrite based on those notes..." —*Joanna Penn, The Creative Penn blog*

Fictional worlds do not exist until writers can vividly describe them on the page. Creative and imaginative descriptions gives the writing a sense of originality and believability, while non-descript details can make the prose seem vague and implausible.

Just remember as your drafting your next masterpiece, the descriptive details a writer includes in a story should serve a purpose, and not just pad the writing with more words.

Sensory details can create concrete images, and they should relate to one or more of the five senses. Many of them can be adjectives, although they can also function as verbs or adverbs, depending on how they are used in a sentence.

The setting is often an afterthought by most writers, but it can have a huge influence and effect on your story. The descriptions of locations, backdrops, or landscapes can even function like an actual character that impacts the plot and emotions of your characters.

So I have an included a bonus list of descriptive words taken from my own personal "scent/smell" database that I've found useful in my own writing for creating stronger scenes, which include the seasons or climate. These descriptors should help writers as much as they've helped me to revise a scene. Please include these lists as a powerful reference tool in your writer's toolbox.

Christmas / Winter:

Pine cones, Fresh-Baked Gingerbread, Mulled Wine, Apple Cider, Fig Pudding, Cranberry, Nutmeg, Cinnamon, French Vanilla, Butter, Baked Ham, Woodsmoke, Bayberry Candles, Orange and Cloves, Peppermint, Roasted Chestnuts, Brown Sugar, Gingerbread, Hot Chocolate, Evergreen, Eggnog, Wet Cedar, Wet Woolen Mittens, Bread Rising And Baking, A Pot of Coffee, Frying Bacon, Spruce Needles, Sage And Thyme, Crisp Smell of Fresh Snow.

Springtime:

Lilacs, Insect Repellent Spray, Suntan Lotion, Corn On The Cob, Watermelon, Cantaloupe, New Hay, Petunias, Charcoal Starter, Seashore, Salty Ocean Breeze, Chlorine, Blueberry

Muffin, Gasoline, Campfires, Lavender, Freshly Cut Grass, Fresh Laundry, Cherries, Melon, Ripe Red Strawberries, Cucumber, Shaving Cream, Talc Powder.

Summer/Warm Weather:

Honey-Suckle, sea drifting inland on the wind, Orange Ice-Cream Bars, Tangerine, Licorice, Bubble Gum, Lemonade, Ice Tea, Perspiration, Cola – Soda, Sea Salt, Fishy, Seaweed or Algae, Coconut Oil, BBQ Sauce, Bamboo, Fresh Sliced Pineapple, Downy April Fresh Fabric Softener, Fragrant Teak Wood, Clean Scent of Cotton, Powdery Musk, Exhaust Fumes, Juniper Bushes, Freshly Cut Flowers, Honey, Inflatable Plastic.

Halloween / Back to School:

Jack-O-Lantern Innards, Candy, Chocolate, Hot Glue, Cornstalks, Damp Leaves, Overturned Earth, Rotting Brown Apples, Roasting Pumpkin Seeds, Chili, Cornbread, Cinnamon, Nutmeg, Tea, Potpourri, Smoking Match, Rain-Soaked Leaves, Distant Fires, Hay, Unpolluted Pure Scent of Rain, Leather, Pencil Lead/Graphite, Dried Corn Kernels Cooking, Wet Dog, Moss, Rotten Wood, Decaying Leaves, Buttery Popcorn, Cotton Candy.

Thanksgiving / Autumn:

Cedar Wood, Bay Rum, Turkey, Scalloped Potatoes, Pecan Pie, Pumpkin Pie, Homemade Rolls, Walnut, Banana Nut

Bread, Cranberry Spice, Green and Musky Scent of Bergamot, key, Scalloped Potatoes, Pecan Pie, Pumpkin Pie, Homemade Rolls, Walnut, Banana Nut Bread, Cranberry Spice, Green and Coffee Cake.

***

When a writer uses evocative writing and their descriptions activate the five senses within your reader or arouse their emotions or vividly impart a mood, they are creating an engrossing and entertaining read.

Now go through your own manuscript and revise your scenes into dramatic, realistic settings by describing the scents and the climate.

CONCLUSION

Quote: "The bestselling writers who endured fifty, or even a hundred rejections, before finally achieving success would make for such a long list of names that I would develop carpal tunnel syndrome just typing them all. Perseverance is as important as talent and craftsmanship." —*bestselling author, Dean Koontz*

Now that you have a clearer idea on how to revise shallower scenes by using the Deep POV technique, search for *telling* sentences or paragraphs and revise them by applying this amazing method, but please avoid using overworked clichés in your writing.

Vivid descriptions will grab a reader's attention and emerge them within your story by *showing* readers your vivid fictional world. Description is a crucial element of powerful storytelling.

In order to avoid the drawbacks of "telling" instead of "showing," please remember these tools:

* *Provoke emotion and mood through vivid descriptions.*

* Apply sensory details to bring scenes to life.

* Use powerful, distinctive verbs, and don't overuse "ly" adverbs.

* Create evocative writing by blending setting with the five senses.

Well, that's it for my advice on writing compelling description. All of these tools and recommendations should really help fiction writers to create vivid and dramatic scenes that will keep readers coming back for more.

A final word of advice…

I've written a lot of books. Some good, and some, well, *not* so good. My first three novels were traditionally published without a literary agent. And I hate to tell you that the advance was dismal and I didn't sell as many books I'd hoped.

Looking back, I know what I did wrong. I didn't have any critique partners. The manuscript wasn't tightened up and polished enough. I didn't hire a professional, freelance editor.

A first or second draft should never, *ever* be what a writer self-publishes. As a matter of fact, the first draft or two should be ruthlessly edited. Personally, I do at least ten or more drafts on my own fiction stories.

Please do not rush to publish your book!

If you have a slower scene that readers might think is boring, but you feel is vital to the plot, then find a way to Deepen the POV and the characterization, and also ramp up the tension.

Learn to self-edit if you can't afford to hire a professional editor. Find a few good critique partners (and if you don't know what this is, then that's a red flag that you might not be ready to self-publish yet), and really take the time to study story structure. I recommend that new writers read books in the genre that you want to write in and dissect them. Devour them. Analyze every aspect of the writing.

Be patient and never stop improving your craft.

As you write, and read, and study, you'll get better at including Deep POV in earlier drafts.

Once you've finished the fifth draft of your manuscript, then you're ready to use the Deep POV method. This is when you will go through each scene and find all the shallower writing and revise the heck of it.

Wishing each and every one you much success on your writing journey!

BONUS MARKETING TIP

Read on for one more chapter with amazing tips on giving your book the perfect title from my inspiring guidebook, which can double your sales within weeks!

HOW TO INCREASE YOUR BOOK SALES IN 30 DAYS

This in-depth marketing guide is perfect for writers publishing their first novel or indie authors trying to gain a wider readership. The manual includes valuable tips on networking, how to get more book reviews, and contains wonderful advice on how to best promote your work from established authors and popular book bloggers.

Whether you're a multi-published author looking to expand your audience or a self-published writer, this book will instantly give you the tools to market your fiction like a pro! Free bonus features include how successful authors use social media to connect with potential readers, reviewers, and how to sell more books.

BOOK TITLES

Here are fifteen ways to create an awesome book title!

These ideas and suggestions on how to pick a unique book title for your next bestseller or untitled work-in-progress (manuscript) should help writers get inspired. I also included a few tips on choosing the right title for your book's genre.

Creating the perfect title can be difficult and nerve-racking. Most marketing experts recommend keeping the title at three words or less, but I suggest no more than five words.

Your book title needs to pop, convey a hint at what your story is about, and if possible, somehow tie into the actual theme. Depending on your genre, here are a few suggestions on creating the perfect book title.

1) Song titles can give you quite a few great book title ideas. Find a band that fits your story's theme and browse the titles of their songs. And even the lyrics can be inspiring.

2) Like watching TV? Do any of the shows you watch have a theme or storyline similar to your manuscript? Browse the titles of each episode to come up with ideas.

3) Use a book title generator to come up with fresh ideas for your novel.

4) Use strong, active verbs and action words that relate to your plot or story theme.

5) To make sure your title is unique, try dropping the "A" or "The" at the beginning. For example: "The Scandalous Affair" can be shortened to: "Scandalous Affair" or "A Fall Through Time" can be shortened to: "Fall Through Time."

6) Scan the titles in the bestseller lists of the genre that your book falls under on Amazon to get ideas. If you write thrillers browse and see what's popular in your genre and sub-genres.

7) Use the main characters first name or mix it with a strong verb. Or use an adjective like Dean Koontz's "Odd Thomas" to gain a reader's interest.

8) Where does your wonderful story take place? Title the book after the town or city. Or the name of the business or character's place of work.

9) What is the theme or overall story conflict? Since my adult paranormal romance dealt with immortals and the climax was centered around an eclipse, I titled my book, *Immortal Eclipse.*

10) One or Two word titles seem to have the most impact on readers and get better sales. Use one or two strong nouns or verbs that describe your story. Whatever you choose, make sure that it is easy to pronounce and simple to remember. Keep the title short and clear-cut.

11) Depending on the genre, the book title could be a play on words or a popular expression. For instance: "Some Like it Cold" or "The Non-Avengers" or "Bertha, The Vampire Slayer."

12) Take the title of a popular movie or book and switch the words up. For instance: "The Baker Who Loved Me" or "Pride and Poison" or "The Fast and the Fighter" or "Five Shades of Red."

13) The title could be a major event or activity from your story-line. For instance: "Apple Bakers" or "Ghost Hunters Unite" or "The Day We Drowned" or "Fairgrounds" or "Chained Up" or even "Housebound."

14) Name the book after the villain or opposing forces. For instance: "The Empire Strikes Back" or "Alien" or "Jaws" or "Hannibal."

15) Before picking a title, I suggest that you Google your title and do an Amazon search to make sure it is unique. The goal is to ensure that your book title stands out against the competition.

I hope that these tips give you some great ideas for titling your next book!

Even if you've already published a few books or you're just starting out in the indie publishing world, there's always more to learn on the craft of fiction and book promotion. If you're determined to take your writing career seriously and make it to the next level, you need to make sure that your author branding and book packaging are "genre specific" to hit your target audience and build a loyal readership.

HUMBLE REQUEST

If you read this handbook and find the tools and tips helpful to improving your own storytelling abilities, please consider posting an honest review on Amazon, Barnes & Noble, or Goodreads.

Word of mouth is crucial for any author's success, and reviews help to spread the book love. So please consider leaving a short (*a sentence or two is fine!*) review wherever you purchased this copy and/or on Goodreads.

If I get enough reviews stating that this guide helped writers to hone their craft, then I'd love to include additional books in this Deep POV series with new topics, such as romance, suspense, and world-building.

And please visit my blog, "Fiction Writing Tools," for tons of helpful advice on book promotion, author branding, and self-editing.

FICTION WRITING TOOLS

Bestselling author S. A. Soule shares her expertise with writers by providing surefire, simple methods of getting readers so emotionally invested in their stories that booklovers will be flipping the pages to find out what happens next.

Each of these helpful and inexpensive self-editing books in the *Fiction Writing Tools* series encompass many different topics such as, dialogue, exposition, internal-monologue, setting, and other editing techniques that will help you take your writing skills to the next level.

THE WRITER'S GUIDE TO CHARACTER EMOTION (Book 1)

Most writers struggle with writing a captivating story. The fastest way to take your writing to the next level is by the use of "Deep Point-of-View" which can transform any novel from mediocre storytelling into riveting prose. This manual will explain how you can greatly enhance your characterization, and how to emerge your readers so deeply into a scene that they'll experience the story along with your characters. Also, learn how to avoid "telling" by applying "showing" methods through powerful examples that will deepen the reader's experience through vivid, sensory details.

THE WRITER'S GUIDE TO DEEP POV (Book 2)

Fastest Way to Improve Dialogue, Settings, and Characterization

No matter what genre you write, this second manual on the Deep Point of View technique should be kept as a vital reference in every writer's toolbox. This in-depth guide offers specific, practical tools for creative fiction writers on how to use the Deep POV method to create realistic settings, visceral responses, and lifelike characters.

Crammed with even more examples and ways to eliminate shallow writing, this book also gives writers invaluable techniques required to master describing facial expressions, body language, "voice," and character emotions. This helpful source of endless inspiration will instantly enhance the reader's experience by explaining how to *dig deeper* to "show don't tell," which is necessary to crafting compelling dialogue, vivid scenes, and deepening characterization.

HOW TO INCREASE YOUR BOOK SALES IN 30 DAYS

Learn How To Sell More Books in a Month!

This in-depth marketing guide is perfect for writers publishing their first novel or indie authors trying to gain a wider readership. The manual includes valuable tips on networking, how to get more book reviews, and contains wonderful advice on how to best promote your work from established authors and popular book bloggers.

Whether you're a multi-published author looking to expand your audience or a self-published writer, this book will instantly give you the tools to market your fiction like a pro! Free bonus features include how successful authors use social media to connect with potential readers, reviewers, and how to sell more books.

HOW TO WRITE ENTICING BOOK BLURBS

An Awesome Product Description Is The #1 Thing You Need To Sell More Books!

Learn how to instantly create an appealing blurb for your book. Writing back jacket copy (blurb or marketing copy) can give most writers a major headache. To write compelling blurbs, writers need strong keywords, a great opening and last sentence "hook," and be able instantly grab a reader's attention within seconds.

A book description (found on the back of a novel or as a marketing tool online) is one of the most important selling tools an author can have for their self-published book. Even if you're a writer sending out query letters to literary agents, then you definitely need a strong enough "hook" to get their attention, and this guide should inspire you.

THE WRITER'S GUIDE TO AUTHENTIC DIALOGUE (Book 4)

A Powerful Reference Tool to Crafting Realistic Conversations in Fiction!

This manual is specifically for fiction writers who want to learn how to create riveting and compelling dialogue that propels the storyline and reveals character personality.

Writers will also learn how to weave emotion, description, and action into their dialogue heavy scenes. With a special section on how to instantly improve characterization through gripping conversations. All of these helpful writing tools will make your conversations sparkle!

THE WRITER'S GUIDE TO PLOTTING A NOVEL (Book 5)

Awesome Tips on Crafting a Riveting "Hook" that instantly Grabs Your Reader

This manual offers amazing techniques for creating stronger beginnings and ways to write a page-turning "hook" for your fiction novel. Writers will learn how to make the first five pages so intriguing that the reader won't be able to put your book down, and reveal how you can successfully craft your first chapter.

Also, writers will get the tools needed to blend character goals with a riveting scene, and how basic plot structure can effectively and instantly strengthen the narrative. Plus, get bonus tips from other bestselling authors, advice on self-publishing a novel, and help with manuscript word counts. Whether you're writing an intense thriller or a sweeping romance, all novels follow the same basic outline described in detail within this book.

ABOUT THE AUTHOR

S. A. Soule is a bestselling author, who has years of experience working with successful novelists. Many of her fiction and non-fiction books have spent time on the bestseller lists.

Her handbooks in the "Fiction Writing Tools" series are a great resource for writers at any stage in their career, and they each offer helpful tips on how to instantly take your writing skills to the next level and successfully promote your books.

The bestselling, "Writer's Guide to Character Emotion," will offer insight into 'showing versus telling' and reveal ways to instantly improve characterization.

Please feel free to browse her blog, which has some great information on creative writing online at: **Inspirational Writing Tips**

16018454R00134

Printed in Great Britain
by Amazon